BARRON'S BOOK NOTES

CHARLES DICKENS'S

Great Expectations

BY

Holly Hughes

SERIES EDITOR

Michael Spring
Editor, *Literary Cavalcade*
Scholastic Inc.

BARRON'S EDUCATIONAL SERIES, INC.
New York / London / Toronto / Sydney

ACKNOWLEDGMENT

We would like to acknowledge the many painstaking hours of work Holly Hughes and Thomas F. Hirsch have devoted to making the *Book Notes* series a success.

International Standard Book No. 0-8120-3414-7

PRINTED IN THE UNITED STATES OF AMERICA

789   550   9876543

CONTENTS

HOW TO USE THIS BOOK

You have to know how to approach literature in order to get the most out of it. This *Barron's Book Notes* volume follows a plan based on methods used by some of the best students to read works of literature.

Begin with the guide's section on the author's life and times. As you read, try to form a clear picture of the author's personality, circumstances, and motives for writing the work. This background usually will make it easier for you to hear the author's tone of voice, and follow where the author is heading.

Then go over the rest of the introductory material—such sections as those on the plot, characters, setting, themes, and style of the work. Underline, or write down in your notebook, particular things to watch for, such as contrasts between characters and repeated literary devices. At this point, you may want to develop a system of symbols to use in marking your text as you read. (Of course, you should only mark up a book you own, not one that belongs to another person or a school.) Perhaps you will want to use a different letter for each character's name, a different number for each major theme of the book, a different color for each important symbol or literary device. Be prepared to mark up the pages of your book as you read. Put your marks in the margins so you can find them again easily.

Now comes the moment you've been waiting for—the time to start reading the work of literature. You may want to put aside your *Barron's Book*

Notes volume until you've read the work all the way through. Or you may want to alternate, reading the *Book Notes* analysis of each section as soon as you have finished reading the corresponding part of the original. Before you move on, reread crucial passages you don't fully understand. (Don't take this guide's analysis for granted—make up your own mind as to what the work means.)

Once you've finished the whole work of literature, you may want to review it right away, so you can firm up your ideas about what it means. You may want to leaf through the book concentrating on passages you marked in reference to one character or one theme. This is also a good time to reread the *Book Notes* introductory material, which pulls together insights on specific topics.

When it comes time to prepare for a test or to write a paper, you'll already have formed ideas about the work. You'll be able to go back through it, refreshing your memory as to the author's exact words and perspective, so that you can support your opinions with evidence drawn straight from the work. Patterns will emerge, and ideas will fall into place; your essay question or term paper will almost write itself. Give yourself a dry run with one of the sample tests in the guide. These tests present both multiple-choice and essay questions. An accompanying section gives answers to the multiple-choice questions as well as suggestions for writing the essays. If you have to select a term paper topic, you may choose one from the list of suggestions in this book. This guide also provides you with a reading list, to help you when you start research for a term paper, and a selection of provocative comments by critics, to spark your thinking before you write.

THE AUTHOR AND HIS TIMES

Dickens is one of the world's best-loved writers, and *Great Expectations* may be Dickens' most autobiographical work. Although an earlier novel, *David Copperfield*, followed the facts of Dickens' life more closely, the narrator David seems a little too good to be true. The narrator of *Great Expectations*, Pip, is, in contrast, a man of many faults, who hides none of them from the reader. If Pip is a self-portrait, Dickens must have been a reservoir of inferiority complexes, guilt, and shame.

Many other aspects of *Great Expectations* are autobiographical, too. The beginning of the novel is set shortly after Dickens' birthdate (1812) in the country of his childhood—the Kentish countryside by the sea (the nearest large town is Rochester, where Miss Havisham lives). Dickens wasn't an orphan, as Pip is, but he may well have felt like one. His parents, John and Elizabeth Dickens, were sociable, pleasant people, but Mrs. Dickens was a careless housekeeper and Mr. Dickens, a minor civil servant, always spent more money than he made. When Charles, who was the eldest boy, was nine, the Dickenses pulled up roots and moved to London to try to live more cheaply. Charles was appalled by the cramped, grubby house they lived in there, and even more ashamed when his father was arrested and taken to debtors' prison. The rest of the Dickenses were allowed to move into prison with their father, but twelve-year-old Charles had to live on his own outside.

His mother arranged for him to get a job in a filthy, rat-infested warehouse, pasting labels on bottles of boot blacking (a kind of shoe polish). This time of his life was so miserable that he never told anyone, not even his own wife or children, about it. He was called "the young gentleman" by the other boys at the factory, who resented his air of being better than they were. But he did feel that he'd come down in life, and he developed a bitter sense of ambition and self-reliance: he vowed never to let himself be poor or in debt again.

This situation lasted only a few months; then John Dickens received an inheritance from a rich aunt (a windfall of money also crops up in *Great Expectations*) and the family moved out of prison. After much pleading, Charles was allowed to quit his job, but he never forgave his parents for making him take it. Yet later, when he grew up and became wealthy, his irresponsible parents blithely sponged off him, until he basically had to disown them. It's no wonder that his books are full of inadequate parents who have warped their children.

After leaving the warehouse, Charles was allowed to return to school, but the schoolmaster was so cruel and malicious that the boy learned almost nothing (his books are full of terrible schools and teachers, too). He felt cheated because he never did get the classical education of an English gentleman; instead, he had to pick up what he could himself, mostly by reading novels and by going to the theater, which he loved his whole life long. For a while he thought about becoming an actor, but acting wasn't a respectable career back then, and Charles desperately wanted to be respectable. Instead, he took a job as a law clerk (lawyers and the complex legal system are often satirized in his novels). From there he went on to become a court reporter, then a newspaper reporter assigned to cover Parliament. This brought him his first reputation, as a political commentator. His talent was obvious and, coupled with his amazing capacity for hard work, fueled by fierce ambition, he rose quickly in the world of journalism. Eventually, he was asked to write his first book of fiction, *The Pickwick Papers*, a loose series of comical sketches which made him an overnight sensation. He was only 25, but from then on everything he did was golden. His novels were always best-sellers, and he was a celebrity, as a movie idol or pop star would be today.

His personal life, however, was not so magical. The first girl he had fallen in love with, Maria Beadnell, teased and flirted with him for a year before she suddenly refused to see him again; on the rebound, desperate to be married, he proposed to Catherine Hogarth, just before his first big success. Catherine was probably a good woman, but she was dull and never understood her brilliant, insecure husband. Although they had ten children, they were never happy together. Twenty-two years later, they finally separated—scandalous behavior for those times, especially for such a public figure as Dickens had become. To add to the scandal, the middle-aged Dickens had fallen in love with a coy, cold young actress named Ellen Ternan, who apparently strung him along heartlessly.

Perhaps this is why Dickens was so eager to hold onto his reading public; he felt closer to them than to his own family and friends. At least his readers always adored him. In the nineteenth century, before radio or television or movies, novels were the main form of popular entertainment. Families read them together by the fireside at night, and even poor people who couldn't read would meet regularly on the street corner or in a tavern to listen to someone reading a book, chapter by chapter, out loud. Dickens had a natural instinct for satisfying this wide audience. He included all levels of entertainment: political satire, flowery romance, weepy melodrama, spine-tingling mystery, and broad slapstick comedy. His cast of characters was drawn from all social classes.

Even though he constantly criticized English society, however, Dickens was too much a man of his time to question the fundamental values of the Victorian age. Like his readers, he believed in a happy family life, Christianity, material prosperity, hard work, and human decency. In his books those are the ingredients of a happy ending.

In his life, those ingredients weren't quite so satisfying—and he couldn't understand why. At the pinnacle of his achievement, Dickens felt that everything he had worked for had turned into hollow and ashy disappointment. In spite of all his political satire, society hadn't changed for the better. Although he was a wealthy man now, it only meant he had to sustain a more expensive lifestyle. He couldn't seem to get close to his children. As a celebrity, he no longer felt he belonged to any social class, or had any real friends. It was in this mood that he commenced writing *Great Expectations* in 1860. But writing brought no release. For the next few years of his life, Dickens increasingly used hard work to stave off depression, but it only ruined his health, and eventually led to his death of a stroke in 1870.

In spite of his depression, Dickens managed to include in *Great Expectations* the irrepressible comedy he was known and loved for. His driving need to please his public kept him on balance. The novel's themes, however, are very serious. He writes about human nature itself, a mixture of misery, joy, hope, and despair. Dickens did not write such a profound novel because his public demanded something heavy; he wrote it because his vision of life was growing complex, and he was too great a genius to simplify it. Luckily, he was also a great enough genius to write a book that people could enjoy. Though Dickens bared his psychological problems in this novel, he was still trying to reach out to his readers, to make them see their own lives more clearly. Perhaps this is why people love Dickens—because he is so human, so honest, and so much like all of us.

THE NOVEL

The Plot

In a village cemetery, a small boy, Pip, is accosted by a runaway convict who demands food and a file to saw off his leg iron. Terrified, Pip steals the items from the home where he has been living with his sister and her husband Joe since his parents died. Soon after, the convict is recaptured when he stops to fight with another fugitive out on the marshes; he protects Pip, however, by saying that he stole the things from the house himself.

Not long after this, Pip is invited to the gloomy home of rich, eccentric Miss Havisham, who wants a boy to "play" for her amusement. But Pip's real role at Miss Havisham's turns out to be as a toy for Miss Havisham's adopted daughter, Estella, who has been raised with one purpose—to break men's hearts, in revenge for the time when Miss Havisham was deserted on her wedding day years ago. Pip falls in love with Estella, and becomes self-conscious about his low social class and unpolished manners. From then on, his abiding dream is to be a gentleman. He is bitterly disappointed when he becomes a teenager and Miss Havisham sees nothing better for him than to become apprenticed to his brother-in-law Joe at his blacksmith's forge. Also at the forge is Orlick, a slouching, belligerent young man who attacks Pip's older sister, Mrs. Joe Gargery, one night, leaving her dumb and paralyzed. Although Pip sees no escape from this path of life, he confesses to Biddy, the village girl who helps care for Mrs. Joe, that he still hopes to become a gentleman and marry Estella.

Then a London lawyer, Jaggers, comes to the village to tell Pip that he has come into a fortune from an anonymous source. Because Pip once saw Jaggers at Miss Havisham's he immediately assumes that she is his secret benefactor and that she intends for him to marry Estella. Pip goes to London to become a gentleman. His tutor is a cousin of Miss Havisham's, Matthew Pocket, whose son Herbert becomes Pip's roommate and best friend. Pip turns his back on Joe and Biddy, embarrassed by his humble roots. Even when he goes home for Mrs. Joe's funeral, he treats them in a condescending manner. In London, he picks up extravagant habits, and both he and Herbert get into debt. When Pip turns twenty-one, however, he gets a regular allowance of five hundred pounds a year; the first thing he does with this is to buy Herbert a partnership in a shipping firm, without Herbert ever knowing who was responsible.

Estella, who is now an elegant young lady, arrives in London to begin to collect and torment suitors. Pip, who sees her often, is outraged when she allows Bentley Drummle, a surly lout from a rich aristocratic family, to hang around her. When he complains to her, however, she reminds him that her goal in life is to attract and humiliate men; Pip is the only one she does not string along, and he should be grateful for that.

One dark stormy night, Pip gets a mysterious visitor: a gruff, grizzled seafaring man. Just as Pip is about to throw him out, he reveals himself as the convict Pip had helped that evening in the cemetery. Then he proudly announces that he is Pip's secret benefactor. After being deported to Australia, he made a fortune, and sent it all back to England to make a gentleman out of that little boy. Pip feels sick at heart, realizing that his fortune didn't come from Miss Havisham after all, and there is no plan to marry him to Estella. More than that, he is mortified to learn that the source of his money is so base. Pip wants to cut off his connection to the convict, Magwitch, as soon as possible. But if the police discover Magwitch has returned to England, he could be put to death. Feeling responsible, Pip helps him hide out.

Magwitch tells Pip and Herbert his history. The convict Magwitch was fighting with on the marshes was his partner, Compeyson, who gave evidence against Magwitch to save his own skin. Pip and Herbert realize that Compeyson is the same man who deserted Miss Havisham on her wedding day. Pip visits Miss Havisham, to tell her he's lost his fortune; Estella is there, and he learns that she's going to marry Drummle. Dejected, Pip returns to London to learn that Compeyson is there, too, and is hunting down Magwitch. Herbert, Pip, and Jaggers' clerk Wemmick hatch a plan to take Magwitch in a rowboat down river, where he can board a ship bound for Germany. Pip agrees to go abroad with Magwitch, since he feels he has no future left in England.

Miss Havisham asks to see Pip one more time. She agrees to complete the anonymous payments for Herbert's partnership, now that Pip has no fortune. Miss Havisham was deeply affected by Pip's outburst to Estella, and she is full of remorse for her selfish scheme; she begs Pip to forgive her. He does so, but just as he is leaving, she bends over the fire and then suddenly goes up in a pillar of flame. Pip rescues her, but she never recovers.

Back in London, Pip learns that Magwitch once had a baby girl, but she was abandoned by her mother. Piecing together evidence, Pip realizes with shock that Estella was that baby girl.

The time comes to take Magwitch away. Two
nights before the departure, Pip receives a mysterious
message to go to his own home village, where he is
attacked by Orlick. Herbert rescues him, but he's still
battered and sore when they set off down the river.
The next dawn, just as they are hailing the German
ship, a police boat pulls out and stops them. Magwitch spots Compeyson, the informer, in the boat and
knocks him overboard. Compeyson drowns, and
Magwitch is taken to prison. Pip, who has grown to
love Magwitch, sticks with him until the old man dies
in prison, before his execution.

Pip falls ill. Joe nurses him through his sickness,
pays his debts, and then disappears, not wishing to
be in his way. Pip now appreciates Joe's loving loyalty
and follows him home, planning to marry Biddy and
settle down; but when he gets there Biddy has just
married Joe. Pip decides to leave, accepting a job in an
overseas branch of Herbert's office.

Returning to England many years later, Pip visits
Miss Havisham's house, which has been pulled
down. Estella is there, too. Her husband Drummle,
who treated her badly, has died. Suffering has given
Estella human feelings at last, and she is kind to Pip.
As they walk away hand in hand, it looks as though
they will finally get together.

The Characters

Pip

Pip is the narrator and the main character of *Great
Expectations*—and possibly also the voice of the author. If Dickens intended Pip as an autobiographical
figure, it's interesting—as a sidelight on Dicken's per-

sonality—that he tried to make Pip so full of flawed qualities. And yet, despite those flaws, Pip emerges as a character we care about very much.

In a way, we feel close to Pip because he isn't trying to impress us or build up his own image; instead he confesses all his shames and fears to us. It's as though, through Pip, Dickens is working out all his worst feelings about himself. Look back over Dickens' life story and compare it to Pip's. When Dickens was working in the blacking warehouse he felt "above it," just as Pip feels above his job, as an apprentice to a blacksmith. When the other boys resented Dickens, he learned to keep to himself—just as little Pip seems to do in Mrs. Wopsle's school. Dickens had one friend, Bob Fagin, whom he ungratefully looked down on, in much the same way that Pip takes for granted his village friends Biddy and Joe. Pip is also a hopeless romantic, beneath all his shyness; he remains obsessed for years with an idealized image of his beloved Estella—who's really proud and cold. In writing this, Dickens may have been chastizing himself for his own infatuations with Maria Beadnell or Ellen Ternan. When Pip first receives his mysterious "expectations" and becomes a gentleman, his shyness and ambition combine to make him a snob; Dickens may be critically reliving his own reaction when he was suddenly hit with fame and fortune at a young age.

Dickens sometimes seems so close to Pip, it's hard for him to give Pip his own identity. Pip is highly impressionable and sensitive to criticism, and so he changes easily—more than other characters in the book. (Some other characters seem to change, but read them carefully—it could just be Pip's attitude to them that's changing.) Throughout the book, Pip struggles to form his identity; he doesn't even seem to have a real name. The first thing we learn about him is that he himself shortened his name, Philip Pirrip, to the insignificant nickname Pip. Philip Pirrip was also his father's name, but the name feels alien to Pip because he never knew his father (some readers have seen the whole book as being Pip's search for a father—which is, after all, another way of searching for identity). When Pip receives his mysterious fortune, one of the terms is that he will always be called "Mr. Pip"—a title that seems vain and ridiculous, as though mocking the idea that a "pip" should ever become important. Even Pip's best friend Herbert Pocket immediately changes Pip's name to "Handel," as though by giving Pip a new name he'll help him change into the gentleman he wants to be.

While we're trying to figure out who Pip really is, we have to remember that he's the narrator—so we can't always trust what he says about himself. (If you wrote a description of yourself, do you really think it would show the whole picture?) Pip is intelligent, intuitive, and, even as a child, unusually observant of the adult world around him. But he has certain blind spots when it comes to himself. He's always telling us how bad he was, how guilty he felt, how everything was his fault, and how sure he was that he was going to be caught and punished. As you read the book, try from time to time to look at Pip as another character might. Set up a moral scale of all the characters, and see how Pip fits in. Look especially at his good qualities—tact, sensitivity, imagination, modesty. You'll have to keep reminding yourself of them, because Pip never mentions them.

Why is Pip so hard on himself? Some readers say it stems from his early upbringing, surrounded by unloving adults like his sister Mrs. Joe, whose philosophy is "spare the rod and spoil the child." Others point out that Pip is telling us all this years later—long after the events in the book—from the perspective of a middle-aged man, who is being critical of his own past mistakes.

Other readers think Pip isn't being harsh on himself at all—just honest, owning up to faults we all have. Though he seems like a nasty little kid and an unpleasant adolescent, these readers point out, Dickens is just giving us a realistic portrait of child psychology. Most small children, like Pip, are likely to lie, cheat, and steal to get around adults; they don't automatically love their elders and they may hate going to school or to church. (If you've ever been a babysitter, you know that all little kids aren't sweet angels.) And adolescents are often like Pip is: painfully self-conscious, critical of their parents and their parents' friends, unsatisfied with their own daily lives, easily taken in by glamorous but undependable friends. This is all just part of growing up. Watching Pip go through these various stages, we may remember the way we acted at the same age—and wince at the memory.

Pip does seem to view the universe in pretty simple moral terms. Things are either good or bad, noble or common, beautiful or ugly. This is in part a result of his romantic nature, which wants everything in the world to be lovely and perfect and feels frustrated when things fall short of this ideal. It's a product of his upbringing, too—he has no real moral training as a child, only strict threats of punishment, so he forms childishly harsh, absolute ideas of right and wrong for himself. This is also a fairly typical way of viewing the world when you're young, and still trying to judge the people around you. But as he grows older, Pip learns that other qualities—sympathy and forgiveness, for example—need to be used to temper moral judgments. Life isn't as simple as he wants to make it.

Pip doesn't act as if he enjoys life very much. He's a loner as a child, surrounded mostly by adults. Our first view of him is in a graveyard, musing over the tombstones, and the fact that he seems so much at home there tells us something about the morbid streak in his personality. When he is later brought to "play" to amuse rich Miss Havisham, the idea is ironic, and yet fitting because she's a grotesque old bird herself. But Pip does seem to have fun sometimes: as a boy out on Sunday afternoons with his brother-in-law Joe; in London, with his friends Herbert Pocket or Wemmick, even with his disreputable dining society, the Finches of the Grove. Underneath his shy manner, he longs for friends, and he learns in the course of the book just how important friendship can be.

Since Pip is the narrator, his personality affects the tone of the book. We follow Pip from a solemn, solitary little boy to a melancholy middle-aged man; as he grows up, we see the events and characters of the novel through his changing eyes. When Pip is very young, he has a child's vivid imagination that visualizes the world around him as a horror story, a fairy tale, or a cartoon comedy. When Pip becomes an adolescent, he becomes more wrapped up in himself and his own self-image. After he receives his "expectations" and moves to London to become a gentleman, he carefully notes and describes how people around him act, because he's trying to learn how to behave in polite society.

Throughout these stages, Pip remains passive; things happen to him, and he reacts to them, but he doesn't do much on his own. This isn't because he's

weak, however; it's mostly because he's shy. Though
he tells us how strongly he feels about various people
or events, we must remember that he presents a
silent, noncommittal face to the world at large. Once
he has learned who brought him that fortune, however, Pip finally has to break out of his shell, to take on
adult responsibility, to lay plans and carry them out.
He begins to ask questions instead of just observing
what goes on; he also has to fight back against the
forces that have molded him. As you read the novel,
note these stages of Pip's development both as a person and as a narrator.

The different elements of Pip's personality seem to
be constantly in conflict. For example, when he first
learns that he has "expectations" of a great fortune,
his mind goes off in a dozen different directions: selfishness, joy, guilt, suspicion, embarrassment, and
fear of his own new future. Take special note when-
ever Pip describes such emotional turmoil. Because
Dickens isn't trying to make Pip look good, he can
show the whole range of selfish, resentful, kind, and
guilty sensations we all experience. Dickens is so brutally honest that we may be tempted to say Pip's a bad
person—until we search our own minds and discover
that they work the same way.

Joe

Pip is the psychological center of the book, but his
brother-in-law Joe Gargery is the moral center. Pip
struggles to be good; Joe simply is good by nature,
without realizing it.

Joe's good-heartedness remains as a standard while
Pip goes through a rainbow of changes. But Joe is not
a perfect hero. He often appears weak, letting himself
be cowed by Mrs. Joe, Pumblechook, and even Miss
Havisham—so that we're surprised when we recall

he's a brawny blacksmith. In certain scenes he seems stupid; at the beginning of the book, he's like another child, whom young Pip feels he's already outgrowing. Joe can be clumsy, shy, and ignorant. Though we may squirm at the way Pip looks down on him, we too are embarrassed by Joe's social blunders. But Joe has moments of dignity, when his instincts make him act nobly. Because he's common and uneducated, he proves that you don't have to be rich and well-bred to be a true gentleman.

Perhaps Pip should follow Joe's example of goodness. But Joe can't teach Pip how to be good, because he isn't consciously virtuous. The few times he tries to tell Pip how to behave, his advice is so mixed up with rambling nonsense that it's hard for Pip—or us—to take him seriously.

While Pip the narrator recognizes Joe's goodness, Pip the character goes on treating him badly. Joe forgives Pip for this; we can admire that, or wish he had more gumption. As you read, think: how would you behave towards Joe Gargery? It's one thing to criticize Pip for being a snob, and another thing to have to live with someone like Joe.

The Convict

In the first vivid scene in the graveyard, the convict appears as a threatening, violent figure to Pip. At the same time, Dickens shows us what Pip does not recognize: the man is cold, hungry, and desolate. Throughout the book, we're unsettled by mingled fear of, and sympathy for, this man.

Notice how the convict seems like a creature from a primitive world of struggle and survival. Some readers have even seen the convict as a psychological symbol of man's evil nature, which Pip is trying to repress in himself. The convict appears on dark, stormy nights. He is often compared to an animal, especially a dog; he also seems like a cannibal, threatening to eat Pip, wolfing down his food. His greed for revenge, his lust to make money, even his gratitude to Pip, are simple savage emotions that seem out of place in Pip's social setting. (It's fitting that he makes his money on the raw frontiers of Australia—the opposite side of the world.)

At the same time, look for the convict's moments of grace. When he is recaptured, he lies to protect Pip. He is inherently noble (from what we learn of his upbringing, it seems he had no choice but to become a criminal). He swiftly stops himself from being "low" (like Joe, his morals are instinctive, not taught). He also shows great courage and loyalty—traits Pip lacks.

The convict, like Pip, is constantly changing his name: Magwitch, Provis, Campbell. He is searching for a son, just as Pip is searching for a father. But he's a risky blend of decency and evil. Should we expect Pip to accept the convict with open arms when he walks back into Pip's life? If Pip's snobbery to Joe is the ultimate test of his weakness, Pip's ability to love the convict becomes the ultimate test of his strength.

Miss Havisham

Dickens piles on the details about Miss Havisham, as if he's irresistibly fascinated by her. The more he describes her, the more intensely she stands out, looming as a weird, powerful image, coloring the mood of the entire book. Pip's hopes and dreams are all associated with this grotesque figure. This has to make us feel skeptical about them.

Miss Havisham is unpredictable. In some scenes she's as crazy as a loon, making startling statements, asking embarrassing pointed questions, issuing imperious commands. And yet there are times when she seems quite sane, a hard-headed businesswoman and a realistic judge of human character (she immediately perceives Joe's goodness, for example). In some scenes she seems like a victim, a prisoner in her own house, surrounded by greedy relatives and haunted by her own obsessions.

We often hear stories about rich eccentric recluses (Howard Hughes, for example) who lead bizarre lives. Maybe we respond to such stories because they show us that money can't buy happiness. Money does not make Miss Havisham happy. We learn that her money made her a prey for an unscrupulous suitor. After he deserted her, money gave her the luxury of wallowing in her disappointment until it literally drove her crazy. Money gives her power over her relatives, Pip, and her adopted daughter Estella, but in the end this power does more harm than good.

As you read, think about what Miss Havisham would have been like if she hadn't been rich or if her hopes hadn't been blighted. Perhaps Pip ought to be warned by her example not to count too much on his "expectations" of money or of love.

Estella

In many ways, Estella is like Pip. Both are orphans, who have led solitary childhoods; both are being educated by a benefactor for a certain purpose—Estella, to break men's hearts; Pip, to be a gentleman. But Pip always sees Estella as being in another world. She seems older than he is, although they're the same age;

he associates her with rare, glittering objects, like Miss Havisham's jewels or the far-off stars (Estella means "star"). He describes her as a queen, or a fairy-tale princess, and yet only once does he include himself as the knight who will carry her away.

Pip tells us that Estella is beautiful—and heartless. Readers have disagreed over whether Estella is truly passionless. She enjoys watching Pip and Herbert fight as boys; she must get some kind of thrill out of it. Perhaps she uses her power over men deliberately, or perhaps she unconsciously sends off sexy signals. Either way, she doesn't seem to enjoy her cruel flirtations. But notice that even when she tries not to seduce Pip, he is still hopelessly trapped. Because of the customs of his age, Dickens could not write openly about sexual attraction, but Estella must have had something more than cold beauty for her to break so many hearts.

Pip can list Estella's faults—she's proud, selfish, cold, cruel, and unloving. But Pip idolizes Estella too much to describe her accurately. To know her as a flesh-and-blood person, we have to study her speeches and actions. It's difficult because she presents such a hard surface. As you read, you'll have to imagine for yourself how she really feels about Pip.

Jaggers

A powerful evil seems to seethe below the surface in lawyer Jaggers. He is dark and secretive, with a repulsive soap scent and a heavy beard showing through his skin. He has a threatening way of biting his forefinger and pulling out his handkerchief. Criminals won't even dare rob him.

Jaggers obsessively washes his hands for a reason: to remove the taint of his scummy business. Jaggers seems to have seen the worst secrets of everybody's soul. The first time he meets Pip, he accuses him of being "a boy." Even on social occasions, Jaggers somehow brings out the worst in people. Jaggers protects himself from this evil by dwelling on the letter of the law. Watch him at work, describing a case with legal skill that somehow avoids the real nature of crime. Jaggers is one in a long line of Dickens' satirical portraits of English lawyers.

But there's more to Jaggers. His clerk Wemmick says he's "deep." During the novel, he deepens from a villain into a complex man. The longer Jaggers is Pip's guardian, the more he disclaims any responsibility for Pip's expectations, as though he's growing concerned for the boy. After he's finished as guardian, he gives Pip advice in an almost fatherly tone.

If Jaggers is a warm, caring human being underneath, why is he hiding it? Some readers explain that Jaggers is a portrait of Victorian repression, that his physical and verbal tics spring from deep psychological conflicts. Others see a man whose human potential has been warped by his work. Still others think he has been totally disillusioned by the vice and corruption he has seen. Whatever else, he is intelligent and worldly wise. He could be a moral guide for Pip—or another warning figure.

Mrs. Joe

Pip's sister keeps a spotless house, but she doesn't know how to make it a home. In her mind, the sole ingredients of child-rearing are a firm spanking and a dose of tar-water. Her apron, which ought to cover a snuggly lap, offers only a bib bristling with pins. Maybe she's deliberately cruel—or maybe she just has mistaken notions of how to run a family.

Pip doesn't have a good perspective on Mrs. Joe, any more than most children do on the adults closest to them. She's simply a tyrant to him, but what can we gather from her speeches and actions? We see her putting on airs for company, playing up to prosperous Uncle Pumblechook, pushing Pip to make the most of his connection with rich Miss Havisham. A longing for something better in life could be stirring in her breast. Consider how such a woman would feel, married to a simple, contented workman like Joe Gargery.

She's enormously energetic and strong—"a fine figure of a woman," Joe calls her. She may have strong emotions, too, locked up behind that armored apron. (Her brother Pip certainly locks up his feelings.) After she is attacked, we're disappointed to see her immobile, silent, cringing. The real Mrs. Joe is gone long before her funeral.

Pumblechook

Dickens' public liked broad comic caricatures, so he always included some. Pumblechook is a stock character: the pompous, bullying hypocrite. Dickens frequently satirized this particular type of person, which he hated.

Pumblechook *is* a caricature. He resembles his name, with his gaping mouth and hair on end as if he had been choked. With real characters, we may speculate on their feelings; Pumblechook doesn't have any, he's there simply to spice up the comic scenes, to irritate Pip, and to display certain character traits in an exaggerated form. As you read, compare Pumble-chook to the other fawners and snobs in the story. Also, compare him, who claims to be Pip's benefactor, to the real benefactors.

Pip is disgusted with Pumblechook throughout the book. Even as a boy, Pip instinctively dislikes the way Pumblechook moralizes and lords it over the family. When Pip's a teenager, his greatest contempt is saved for Pumblechook's preening, possessive manner. True, Pip's snobbery may sharpen his original dislike of the man. Once Pip has reformed, we should per-haps expect him to treat Pumblechook better—but no. At the end of the book, Pumblechook is still hor-rible, patronizing and insulting Pip at the same time. Pip can't help being rude to him. And somehow we can't blame him; there are always some people who really deserve to be hated, and Pumblechook is one of them.

Herbert Pocket

When Pip first meets Herbert—"the pale young gentleman"—at Satis House, he's like a breath of fresh air there. Herbert is definitely from a different class than Pip; he wants to box, not wrestle, using rules Pip never heard of. But he's not a snob; he's cheerful, forthright, and generous. Later we learn of his faulty upbringing, with a title-chasing mother and absent-minded father, so we admire his sane good sense all the more for surviving unscathed.

In London, Herbert becomes Pip's best friend, the first peer Pip can share things with. Herbert is a good example of a gentleman for Pip to follow. Herbert tact-fully corrects Pip's manners and introduces him to a new way of life. Unfortunately, Pip's money is stronger than Herbert's good influence, and both young men run into debt.

Pip and Herbert are kindred spirits, but they also contrast in many ways. Compare Pip's and Herbert's attitudes toward Miss Havisham, towards Estella, and towards love. Compare Herbert's "expectations" (of becoming a great merchant) to Pip's, and then compare their respective benefactors.

Although he has common sense, Herbert will stick with Pip in spite of his faults, and will risk real danger for him. Pip can learn more than table manners from Herbert Pocket.

Wemmick

Like Pumblechook, Jaggers' clerk Wemmick is a caricature—but Dickens handles Wemmick with affection. He looks like a cartoon, with his square wooden face, a mouth like a mail-box slot, and the morbid rings, brooches, and mementoes he wears. He has certain slogan phrases—"portable property," "the aged parent," "Walmouth sentiments." Whereas Pumblechook is full-blown from the start, Wemmick grows on us, as more details are added to the caricature. Compare our first "professional" view of him—hard, cynical, practical—to our first glimpse of his "personal" side—friendly and frivolous. In later scenes, we see Wemmick's comical house, comical family, and comical ladyfriend. We also see his liveliness at the office, with his crazy fondness for the plaster casts of Jaggers' criminal clients.

How should we view Wemmick's sharply divided life? It may be a kind of sad schizophrenia, or it may be an exaggeration of the way most people behave—a survival tactic. (Compare how Jaggers is eaten up by his work.)

Though he's absurd, Wemmick is a good friend to Pip. Like Herbert, he's cheery, resourceful, and loyal. Pip's friendship with Wemmick tells us that Pip is not so much of a snob as he thinks he is. As an eccentric figure, Wemmick highlights certain character traits. Consider Wemmick's care for his father, his acceptance of the human degradation at Newgate, his light-hearted attitude toward love and marriage; compare these to Pip's attitudes. Wemmick rises above his life's problems. Pip could learn something from that.

Biddy

Biddy is "the girl next door" whom Pip overlooks for Estella. She's Pip's only friend at school. Pip knows she has always loved him. He pays her some attention when he's an apprentice; years later, he thinks he'll marry her to regain a quiet, contented life. All along, he takes her for granted.

Biddy is another orphan; like Estella, she seems older than Pip. Biddy, however, is motherly, even as a child. She brings this much-needed warmth to the Gargery house after Mrs. Joe's attack. Biddy has Joe's clear moral sense, but she adds spunk. She isn't always sweet; she's brutally honest with Pip, even when it hurts her chances with him. As she grows closer to Joe, she becomes more critical of Pip, and has a hard time forgiving him. Thus, even though Joe forgives Pip, Biddy's reaction shows us how much Pip really hurt him.

As you read, compare Biddy to Mrs. Joe, Estella, and Miss Havisham to figure out Dickens' womanly ideal. Then contrast Biddy to Pip. If Pip had stayed at the forge, he probably would have married her. Would he have been better off? Would she?

Drummle

Pip dislikes Bentley Drummle when they are both students at Matthew Pocket's. Drummle is rich and upper-class; this should warn Pip not to aspire towards that class. Drummle isn't really evil, but he has no good points. He's bulky, stupid, bad-mannered, and humorless, in many ways the direct opposite of Pip. Jaggers likes him, perversely, but even so he admits that Drummle's no friend for Pip.

Why is Pip so upset by Drummle courting Estella? He says it's more than jealousy—Drummle is such a boor, he shouldn't touch Estella's brightness. Pip, however, is unable to separate Estella from this base creature. Some people think Drummle is Estella's just reward. Others think his role in the book is as a necessary evil, to make her suffer and become human.

Orlick

Orlick is a figure of purely irrational, unredeemable evil. We see him mostly at night, solitary, slouching in the shadows, drunk or sullen. At the forge with his hammer he looks like the devil in person. He also gives an impression of great physical power. Compare him to other "bad" characters: Pumblechook, the convict, Compeyson, or Drummle.

Orlick attacks Mrs. Joe out of twisted spite, and attacks Pip out of a grudge blown out of all proportion. He robs Pumblechook out of random malice. He seems to enjoy committing these crimes, too, drawing them out with vicious pleasure. He loves violence and doesn't need a logical reason for it.

Yet Orlick keeps escaping and pops up in almost every subplot. If we take Orlick as a symbol of evil, Dickens must be saying that evil is illogical, all-present, and impossible to contain.

Other Elements

SETTING

The first part of *Great Expectations* is set in the marsh country of Kent, where Dickens spent his happy early childhood. Some readers believe that Dickens saw this countryside as a land of childhood innocence for Pip; others point to his descriptions of it—dark, foggy, with low leaden horizons—to show that it is a land of bleak prospects and murky moral views. Whatever it means symbolically, it does create a dramatic atmosphere, almost like an old black-and-white movie, with stark lighting, tilted camera angles, and minimal scenery.

When the scene shifts to London, the somber black-and-white film seems to give way to a grainy color movie, shot with a jostled, hand-held camera. We see faces everywhere, we hear street sounds, we read specific place names. Dickens knew every corner of London; showing it to us through Pip's eyes, he emphasizes that it is dirty, cramped, and chaotic, but we can sense his fascination with it.

The novel moves back and forth between these two locales and two moods, shifting more quickly as it heads toward the climax. Notice that, rowing with Magwitch, Pip follows his life in reverse, from London back to the grim coastal marshes.

Dickens the theater lover also creates in this book two masterful stage sets: Satis House and Wemmick's Castle. Both are described in minute, eccentric detail. Miss Havisham's house tries to shut out life and resist change—yet whites still turn yellow, mice and beetles scuttle about, weeds push through the pavement. Wemmick's home, in contrast, is almost too full of life, of overflowing creative energy. Both houses are examples of mad excess, and Dickens makes them as bizarre as possible.

THEMES

Although *Great Expectations* is more unified than most of Dickens' novels, it still has a number of themes, interwoven in several subplots.

1. GREAT EXPECTATIONS

The title of the book is ironic, for all that Pip hopes for turns to dust. Look at how Pip's disappointment is repeated in the plots of Miss Havisham, Magwitch, Estella, and (in reverse) Herbert. What moral is Dickens expressing here? He may be telling us: a) wealth can corrupt people; b) don't get taken in by promises, hope, and dreams; or c) life will inevitably disappoint you.

2. MONEY

Money has a tricky value in this novel. It is not bad in itself; it helps Herbert, and it saves Pip from debtors' prison. But money can be dangerous. Pip and Miss Havisham both become prey for greedy people because they are wealthy. Also, people who love money too much lose their moral bearings; Pip is the most obvious example of this, but also consider the Pockets. If people don't love money itself, they may love the power it brings, and this can be destructive. For example, money gives Miss Havisham and Magwitch power to ruin their adopted children by molding them in certain images.

3. THE VALUE OF WORK

Some readers have said that Dickens was not criticizing money, only money that doesn't come from hard work. Pip is morally weakest when he's rich and idle; after he reforms, he becomes hard-working. Joe accepts money from Miss Havisham to make Pip an apprentice, but not from Jaggers to let Pip be a gentleman. Joe, whose money is earned honestly, can pay off Pip's gentleman's debts. Herbert, who works hard as a clerk, deserves to become a partner. But Drummle, Estella, and Miss Havisham, who inherit their wealth, are unhappy. On the other hand, Magwitch worked hard for his money and it's still cursed. Jaggers works so hard that it takes over his life, and yet this brings him no satisfaction.

4. PARENTS

This is a book full of orphans, adoptive parents, guardians, and failed parent-child relationships. Pip has many "fathers"—Joe, Magwitch, Jaggers, and Pumblechook—but none of them can give him all he needs. One thing Dickens shows us is the effect parents have on their children. Some children are warped by bad parents—Pip, Estella, Magwitch—yet others like Joe and Herbert have survived bad parents, so perhaps it's unfair for a child to blame them for his own failings. Dickens also looks at the responsibility children have towards their parents. Consider how Pip and Estella treat their various "parents"; but also look at what Wemmick and Clara do for theirs.

5. HUMAN TIES

Many characters in this book are cut off—physically or spiritually—from human companionship. Young Pip, Estella, and Jaggers seem crippled by their locked-up feelings; solitude allows Miss Havisham and Orlick to become psychotic. Contrast them to Dickens' sociable characters, Joe, Herbert, Wemmick, and Wopsle. Largely through them, Pip learns to form bonds of love and loyalty which prove more satisfying to him than the bonds of duty and money. In the end, friendship saves his soul (figuratively) and his life (literally). Pip is bound by one other human tie—to Estella. This is destructive, yet even so Dickens seems to find something fine in Pip's helpless, constant love.

6. GOOD AND EVIL

Many great novels depict the struggle between opposing forces of good and evil; *Great Expectations* depicts good and evil as inseparably intermingled. Pip, with his childishly strict moral views, partitions life into absolutes: Estella is good, Magwitch is bad; Jaggers' world is evil, Herbert's is good. But he must finally learn to accept that all life is mixed together, that you have to find the good along with the bad in people. Look at other divisions in the book: professional vs. personal, gentleman vs. commoner, revenge vs. forgiveness. As we read, we discover that categories blur and opposites turn into each other. This makes all the themes in the novel infinitely complex.

STYLE

Dickens engineers emotional effects in this book by shifting writing styles. He alternates broad effects with subtle touches. Comic exaggeration, satiric understatement, the brooding tones of melodrama, and the stern notes of tragedy all slip in and out. Although he must work through his narrator, Pip, Dickens fine-tunes the tone of Pip's voice to steer our sympathies in certain directions.

Pip's usual voice is quiet and thoughtful; he's even a little stiff and tends toward formal turns of phrase. But he also uses deadpan humor (read the opening two paragraphs); he lashes out at himself (read the end of chapter 8); every once in a while he steps aside and comments wisely on life (read the end of chapter 9). At other times (as in chapter 14) he bursts forth to describe his feelings, with long, rhythmic sentences, urgent questions, and echoing phrases.

Sometimes Pip fades into the background and simply observes, so that Dickens can write scenes ready-made for the stage. Look at some of Estella and Miss Havisham's confrontations, for example; Pip records what is said, adding the actors' gestures and tones of voice, but he doesn't analyze. He doesn't need to, because the dialogue itself, like the dialogue in a TV soap opera, effectively conveys so much passion. Pip interjects comments during some scenes, such as those with the convict, where the drama lies in the twists and turns of Pip's own reactions. He treats other scenes in a vivid overview; describing Wopsle's Hamlet (chapter 31), for instance, he paraphrases what is said and tosses out jumbled details, to make it look as absurd as possible.

In some descriptive passages, Pip works slowly and carefully, anxious to get every detail exact and then to interpret them, as when he first sees Miss Havisham's house (chapter 8). He dashes off other scenes with exaggerated, surreal comic vision, as when he's at the cheap hotel (chapter 45); or he paints a vast landscape in confident, rhythmic prose, as when he sketches the river traffic (chapter 54). These various descriptions are almost like movie shots: the slow close up, the quick take, or the majestic panoramic sweep. Dickens, of course, never saw a movie, but he instinctively used the same techniques to maximum effect.

POINT OF VIEW

Dickens handles the first-person narration skill-fully. In some scenes, especially when he's a boy, Pip relates his exact feelings at the time, without any perspective. In other scenes, especially when he's an adolescent, the sadder-but-wiser Pip, who has already lived through all this, looks at his younger self critically, and comments upon him. Pip is merely a bystander in other scenes, so that we can eavesdrop with him on satiric comedy (as with the Pocket family dinner in chapter 23) or witness melodramatic passion (in various scenes with Miss Havisham and Estella).

Dickens has to stick to Pip's view of the action. When he needs to include events Pip couldn't have witnessed, he has other characters narrate a scene or explain the facts. These additional narrators add to the variety of tones in the novel; each one speaks with a distinctive voice, from Biddy's low-key account of Mrs. Joe's death (chapter 35) to Magwitch's action-packed tale (chapter 42).

Readers have disagreed about how much of Dickens there is in Pip. As you study different passages, consider whether Pip's words simply show what he, the character, is like, or whether you think Dickens is speaking to us through Pip.

FORM AND STRUCTURE

Great Expectations was written in 36 weekly installments, to appear in the magazine *All the Year Round* (Charles Dickens, editor). Some critics have pointed out that Dickens benefited from publishing in installments, because it forced him to keep the action moving along and to keep the subplots inter-connected. Notice how often Dickens ends a weekly number on a note of suspense or excitement. Notice, too, how he manages to bring up different strands of the plot in each number, instead of going off on one track too long.

On the other hand, watch for numbers which consist of only one chapter. Usually these focus on Estella or Magwitch, those two figures Pip tries to keep apart from the rest of his life.

Once the magazine had published the final episode, the novel was brought out in book form, in three volumes, corresponding to the three stages of Pip's expectations. It may help you to look at the outlook and the pattern of action in each of these parts.

Part I When Pip is a boy, life is seen through a boy's eyes; it is a world of monsters and magic, where events happen suddenly and illogically and people behave in unaccountable ways.

Part II This shows Pip as a young "man of the world"; it is much more concerned with developing characters, with social satire, and with financial and legal arrangements.

Part III Pip must become an active member of society. The plot turns into a full-fledged detective story as Pip unravels the secrets around him and hatches a scheme to smuggle Magwitch safely out of the country.

The Story

Dickens wrote *Great Expectations* in weekly installments, each a chapter or two long. Let's take a closer look at the novel, reading it section by section, as it appeared originally. At the end of each weekly number, stop for a moment to savor the note of surprise, or suspense, or foreboding with which Dickens has ended it—and imagine how you'd feel if you had to wait another week to find out what happens next.

PART I

CHAPTERS 1 & 2

When Dickens first thought up the story of *Great Expectations*, he described it to a friend as a "grotesque tragi-comic conception." The elements of tragedy and comedy are tangled together from this first chapter onwards.

Look at how Dickens introduces us to his main character and narrator. The strongest points he makes are that the boy is an orphan and that he has a vivid imagination. Because he has no parents, Philip Pirrip has had to forge his own identity; he first did this by naming himself Pip. He pictures the family he never knew from their tombstones. He's a tragic figure of a lonely little boy hanging around an empty cemetery, but at the same time he's got a comical way of describing his imaginative ideas.

Dickens plunges quickly into his first scene—the incident on which the whole plot is based. A sweeping view of bleak marshland finally focuses on the boy, shivering with fear as well as cold. Then, swift and unexpected, a violent figure looms up from the graves. The convict is described in broken sentences, disconnected glimpses that show how threatening—and pitiful—he is. He barks sharp questions at Pip, and demands food and a file to get the iron off his leg. Read the convict's long speech to Pip; the short pressing phrases, the constant repetitions, are like thumbs tightening on the boy's throat. Yet when he talks about the vicious "young man" who is his accomplice, we guess he's bluffing desperately. As Pip trots away, we hear the convict mutter, "I wish I was a frog. Or an eel!" He's only human.

Although Pip really is scared, Dickens lets little comic touches keep bubbling up. When the convict turns Pip upside down, the church steeple peeks out ludicrously beneath his feet. Pip, thinking he has to be polite to this ruffian, keeps sticking dutiful, irrelevant little comments into the dialogue. The comedy, however, mostly works like hysterical laughter, to emphasize the tension.

NOTE: The Use of Dialect   The convict speaks in a lower-class dialect—"pint" for point, "wittles" for victuals (food)—with contractions and phonetic spellings reminding us how he pronounces everything. Dickens often uses dialect to show class distinctions. As you read, notice who speaks dialect, and how these characters are placed on the social scale.

As Pip looks back at the convict, the man seems small and miserable, heading towards a silhouetted gallows. While the sight of the gallows may make us feel sorry for him, it makes Pip more terrified, for he imagines the convict as a dangerous pirate risen from the dead. Pip, having frightened himself, runs home in a panic. Remember how you felt when you were a little kid, running from monsters in the dark?

The somber tone of this chapter now switches to tongue-in-cheek irony. The mix of tragedy and comedy is reversed in the next chapter; comedy is the major style, while subtle details suggest how miserable Pip's life really is.

NOTE: On Christmas   This is Christmas Eve—a holiday Dickens often wrote about. Today, we think of a classic Dickensian Christmas as a jolly day, with mistletoe, plum pudding, and a twinkling tree. But in this household, there isn't much Christmas cheer. Dickens may be saying that this home is so grim, even Christmas isn't happy. But, now that he is near the end of his career, he could also be disillusioned with the idea of a merry Christmas.

Pip's sister, Mrs. Joe, is a joyless ogre, but she's a familiar ogre to Pip, and so he describes her as a caricature, with her grated skin, her bib full of pins, her cane Tickler, and her stock phrase about bringing up Pip "by hand." Her husband Joe, too, seems like a comic character, the loveable fool, as much a child as Pip is, and certainly just as terrorized by Mrs. Joe.

The whole scene is slapstick. Pip ducks behind the door as Mrs. Joe storms in; Joe makes faces and winks at Pip as they eat; Pip slides a hunk of bread-and-butter for the convict down his pants, and goes through contortions keeping it there all evening. When Mrs. Joe knocks Joe's head against the wall, it's like a cartoon: it doesn't seem as if it would hurt.

Still, there's nothing funny about Pip's guilt as he steals what the convict asks for. Some readers have said his conscience is bothering him; others say he's just a practical little kid, afraid of being caught and punished. He's obviously wrought up, as his imagination turns tiny sounds and sensations into reminders of the convict outside, or signs that he has been found out. In the dead of night, every object he takes from the pantry stands out in sharp detail.

NOTE: Prison Ships   Pip learns from his sister what those prison ships are doing anchored just off the shore. This book is set in the first years of the nineteenth century, when some convicted criminals were still shipped abroad to live in penal colonies. How-

ever, this practice had ended in 1852, a few years
before Dickens wrote *Great Expectations*.

CHAPTERS 3 & 4

As Pip runs out onto the marshes, the gloomy
mood of tragedy falls on the story again. The mists
reflect Pip's moral uncertainty. The spooky fog makes
him imagine accusing figures at every turn; it also
hides the straight path (a symbol of virtue) which Pip
would follow on Sunday (a holy day) with Joe, his
guardian and friend.

In this confusing mist, Pip approaches the wrong
man out on the marshes. This second convict is not as
sympathetic as yesterday's; wordlessly, he hits Pip
and runs away. When Pip finds ''his'' convict, the
man seems in comparison more human than before:
cold and wet, nervous, ravenously hungry, with a
pathetic click in his throat. Pip shows his better side,
too, as he treats the convict kindly. When Pip mentions the other convict, however, the man becomes
violent again, hitting himself and chafing his own leg
as he files his manacle. In spite of a moving speech
about his wretched night of waiting, he's still a dangerous criminal. The eerie sound of the file rasping
through the mists haunts Pip as he slips away.

Pip now believes that he too is a criminal. Back in
the slapstick world of the Gargery house, he expects a
policeman to be waiting there to collar him. His agi-
tation goes unnoticed, luckily, beside Mrs. Joe's vig-
orous preparations for Christmas dinner. But Pip feels
treated like a criminal, gulping breakfast with Joe,
putting on his prisonlike Sunday clothes; the sermons
at church have a powerful effect on his aggravated
conscience.

In Pip's guilty frame of mind, he sees everything around him sharply. He notices his sister's hypocrisy in not going to church herself, and at dinner he gives us devastating capsule descriptions of the adult guests, especially Uncle Pumblechook. He observes the dinner from a child's perspective, stuck at the corner of the table with Pumblechook's elbow in his face, Mr. Wopsle's nose wagging at him, and Joe apologetically spooning gravy for him every few minutes. But although he tries to stay out of their conversation, they focus their attention on Pip. He may be exaggerating this because he feels guilty, but if they really do lecture him like this, it's no wonder he's such a nervous child.

NOTE: Dickens' Use of Satire Dickens certainly plays up the scene for satiric effect. Watch how each person, like a mechanical doll, repeats his or her own obsession or favorite expression. Dickens ruthlessly exposes them, and yet because Pip describes it innocently, the characters simply satirize themselves with every word.

Just as the comedy works up to a high pitch, Pumblechook asks for the brandy, which we know Pip stole. Pip's suspense is painful but comic, as he clutches the table leg. Several recent incidents slide together, for Pumblechook discovers that the bottle, which Pip thought he refilled with water (such a careful little crook), was really refilled with Mrs. Joe's vile tar-water that Pip and Joe had to drink. Pumblechook deserves to choke, of course, and Mrs. Joe deserves being embarrassed. But though Pip may deserve to be discovered, he isn't; inexplicably, Pumblechook passes over the incident. There is no rest for the guilty, however, and when Pumblechook calls for the pork pie, Pip's agony returns doubled. Dickens plays the scene for all it's worth, drawing out this spell of suspense more slowly than the first, each comment and gesture looming large. Then, just when Pip can take no more—bang! a bunch of soldiers bursts in the door with a pair of handcuffs. Disrupting the holiday feast so suddenly, this is like an apparition of Pip's guilty mind come to life.

CHAPTER 5

Once again, Pip magically escapes being found out. The soldiers are not here for him; they need to have their handcuffs fixed by the blacksmith. As Joe steps into his forge, he seems a responsible adult for the first time. Indeed, everybody shows another side; strict Mrs. Joe liberally hands out drinks, Pumblechook is jolly, and the terrifying soldiers turn out to be a bunch of goofs, puffed up with the excitement of their hunt for the convicts (especially the sergeant, so aware that he's working for the King).

Pip does a sort of moral flip-flop, too; watching these law-abiding people enjoying themselves, he has a rush of sympathy for "his" convict, shivering out on the marshes, waiting to be caught. Even though Joe and Pip join the man-hunt, they do so only out of curiosity, and they really feel on the side of the underdogs, the convicts. Although Pip has felt isolated from Joe by his guilt, they're allies again now.

NOTE: Pip and Joe   Watch throughout the novel Pip's fluctuating relationship with Joe, and how sensitive he is to it. It's one of the most important ways we can measure Pip's changing character.

We move out into the dreary desolate landscape of tragedy again—fiercer this time, with a blood-red sunset. In this world of struggle and survival, Pip feels vulnerable, whisked along on Joe's back; we realize afresh that Joe is a big strong man and Pip is still a small boy. Pip knows, helplessly, that he may get in trouble too if the convict is captured. But there's no stopping the man-hunt, with its galloping pace, far-off cries, and helter-skelter paths. The description is disjointed and confused, like a real chase. And it ends abruptly, when they stumble upon the pair of convicts, locked in a furious fight.

After all this action, it's ironic that the convicts are so much more involved in their own fight that they're actually glad to see the soldiers. Pip's convict seems half mad, with his greedy laugh and incoherent boasts. How do we feel about him here? Some readers have been awed by his passion for revenge; others admire how brave and strong he seems, compared to his enemy; others believe this just proves he's a violent criminal. At any rate, the scene's so intense that we forget Pip—until his convict fixes a long perplexing look at him.

The breathless action winds down gradually. The prisoners stop being figures of crime and passion, and appear exhausted, limping and shivering. Then, Pip's convict is transformed again, into a figure of dignity and goodness: he works out a way to get Pip off the hook, by confessing to having stolen the food and the file himself. Pip makes no comment on this act of grace; either he is overwhelmed or too shy to comment, or he is confused by it. Joe, however, immediately forgives the man for stealing from him. Joe is deepening from a comic figure into a real person.

In our final view of the convict, now that he's caught, we look on him with pity. Rowed away by callous fellow prisoners, he heads for a ship which is itself chained up. The reference to Noah's Ark is grimly ironic, for this ship carries no hopeful new life. The final sentence makes us feel that the convict is gone, for better or worse.

CHAPTERS 6 & 7

For a small boy, Pip is capable of some pretty complicated moral reasoning. Notice how convoluted his language gets, too, while he's trying to work his way out of this dilemma. He has gotten away with his crime, but now he has to live with the secret. Some readers say that Pip's conscience is so strong, he is punishing himself with worry. Others point out that Pip has no remorse about stealing from Mrs. Joe; he's just worried that he'll never be able to look Joe in the face again.

Is Pip being a little hypocrite to deceive Joe? Maybe, but at least he has enough good judgment to understand how valuable Joe's trust is. The language turns simple when he tells us that he loves Joe. In rhythmic sentences, all beginning with "That," Pip views his daily routine, in which Joe plays such a big part. Yet the older Pip who narrates this comments bitterly on his decision to go on lying. He criticizes this tendency in human nature, but he comes down hardest on himself.

Gentle comedy follows this serious note. In the heat, light, and noise back home, Pip has a loopy, slightly scrambled view of the company; while this satirizes them, it also expresses exactly what things look like when you're kept up long past your bedtime.

The first chapters all take place in just a few hours. In Chapter 7 Dickens widens his time scope, and shows us Pip's ongoing life. Pip's ironical tone signals a shift to satire. He describes simple things in formal language, giving us a view of himself as an overly serious child. He tells how he, as a child, misinterpreted certain adult phrases and actions. While this pokes fun at those concepts, it also reminds us how young Pip still is at this point.

Dickens often satirized education; here he goes after Mrs. Wopsle's school. Her name sounds like "wobble" or "lopsided," and that's what the school's like.

NOTE: The Meaning of Names   Dickens frequently made up ridiculous names for his characters, names with buried puns or names that have a certain suggestive sound. As you meet new characters in the book, think about what qualities their names express.

Pip's struggle to learn is vividly represented by physical battle with the alphabet and numbers. Dickens exaggerates this to show how very real this battle is for little kids, and how impossible it is for them to pick it up without any help. Pip's letter to Joe is clumsy and poorly spelt—it even contains dialect (which we haven't heard in Pip's speech). As Joe admires Pip's writing, Pip realizes that Joe can't read or write, another measure of how Pip is passing him by. Joe's ignorance and his attempts to sound profound keep cropping up in the dialogue. But satire fades to the background as Joe movingly relates his own wretched childhood, and explains why he gives in to Mrs. Joe. He is not a dumb beast: his simple, unquestioning love for the little boy is his main purpose in life. Joe's hearthfire casts a warm glow; notice how Joe is attached to the fire throughout the book. Yet outside, the cold night wind begins to whistle, and Pip is already looking out the window to the marshes and the stars.

Then the mood changes abruptly. Mrs. Joe and Pumblechook, looking self-satisfied, break sharply in with big news: Pumblechook has arranged for Pip to go "play" for Miss Havisham—who, they plot, will "make" Pip's fortune. Pip knows she's the local rich eccentric, but he can't imagine why he should go there. He has no choice, however; like a prisoner, he's stuffed into his suit, and Mrs. Joe gives him a bath so rough it feels like punishment. (Notice the vivid detail of her wedding-ring, supposedly a symbol of love, scraping harshly over his face.) The stars he looked out at before now shine down unhelpfully as he drives away with Pumblechook.

CHAPTER 8

Dickens begins this chapter with a satiric portrait of Pumblechook, a crass merchant who keeps his seeds (a symbol of life) shut away. The only breakfast conversation he can think of is to call out sums for Pip to do. He and the other merchants on the street are obsessed with business; this is Pip's welcome to life in the big town, Rochester.

Then we come to the meat of the chapter: Pip's introduction to Miss Havisham. Her house is barred outside, like a prison, and a beautiful girl, Estella, appears with the keys to it. When she's rude to Pumblechook, she immediately appears powerful to Pip.

She taunts Pip, too, but from the first moment he is awed by her beauty, her poise, and her superior manner.

Outside, the grounds are empty, windy, and overgrown; inside, the house is unnaturally dark, lit only by Estella's candle. Then Pip enters Miss Havisham's room—entirely candlelit, even in daytime, which would be a wild extravagance in those days before electricity. Pip's vision slowly travels around the unfamiliar furnishings, until it halts, shocked, at Miss Havisham, seated by her dressing-table mirror.

NOTE: The Mirror The mirror not only symbolizes her vanity, it also gives us a double image of her to look at. Pip describes her twice: the first time, all white and elegant—though the white hair feels strange—but the second time, all withered and grotesque. Perhaps the horrible side of it can't sink in at first; or maybe Dickens wants us to see the vision of youth and beauty shrivel before our eyes.

Pip compares Miss Havisham to a skeleton, using a child's symbol of death to get at the impression she makes of being opposed to life. The other important impression is that time is frozen here; she seems in the middle of busy preparations, and yet the clocks have all stopped at 20 minutes to nine.

Miss Havisham deliberately tries to shock Pip, as she commands him to play. But for once, Pip is honest; he's as polite to her as he was to the convict, but he knows he cannot play here, now. (Remember what a serious, unplayful child he is.) Estella returns to play cards with Pip. But the real game is just beginning. Estella insults him over and over; Miss Havisham gleefully probes Pip, to discover that, humiliated as he is, he's already fatally attracted to the girl.

Pip plays into Miss Havisham's scheme as perfectly as if he had been coached for it. He seems to let himself be sucked into this bizarre atmosphere. He's young, highly impressionable, and hasn't developed much moral judgment—so it's no surprise that he falls immediately, unquestioningly, under the spell of Satis House. Miss Havisham may be corpse-like and frightening, but remember, Pip is a boy who grew up in a cemetery.

Daylight hits Pip hard, but he doesn't see the world in its former light. He cries when Estella leaves him, not because he's weak, but because this place has affected him so strongly. His older-self narrator for once doesn't blame him, but explains how he could not help being such a sensitive child. He gets a view of the brewery now (note that Miss Havisham is from a commercial fortune, not nobility, and the sour smell of beer is like a taint on her money).

Pip's overwrought imagination shows him Estella's image everywhere. When she walks on the empty casks in the brewery, it's like another hallucination, the way she floats, disdainful and solitary, above the ground. But inseparable from this beautiful figure is the grotesque figure of Miss Havisham which Pip imagines, hanging by the neck. Romance and horror are yoked together here, just as comedy and tragedy are elsewhere. When Pip finally leaves, he's unbearably depressed. With the convict, his guilt was over a real deed; now his self-doubt is vaguer, more general—and a lot more intense.

CHAPTERS 9 & 10

After the haunting atmosphere of Satis House, Pip's home seems more than ever a slapstick world, where people act out their habitual quirks: Mrs. Joe knocks Pip up-side the wall, and Pumblechook, looking fishy and bloated, gives Pip sums as a warm-up before grilling him about Miss Havisham.

NOTE: Pip's Lie   Why does Pip lie about what he saw? Some readers believe Pip's cool, competent lies prove he's morally flawed. Some say he instinctively protects that magical other world from being soiled by his own world, separating the beautiful from the common. He says he's afraid these people won't understand Miss Havisham—as though he understands her completely already.

The story Pip substitutes is just as incredible. His imagination is impressive; this isn't a clichéd description, but one full of details so wild—and so precise— that you almost feel he couldn't have made it up. For example, notice the cupboard full of pistols, jam, and pills—they don't go together at all, and yet he makes you see them clearly. The final touch is when Pip doesn't lie about the one detail, the candlelight, which Pumblechook can verify—so the whole story is accepted.

But Pip does regret lying to Joe—as before, he feels a different moral obligation towards him than towards Mrs. Joe. While Pumblechook and Mrs. Joe look greedy and bad, plotting to cash in on Pip's good fortune, Joe looks pathetic, trying to join in their discussion. This time, Pip decides to admit to Joe that he has lied. He gets him alone in the forge (by the fire, Joe's symbol) and blurts out the truth. He goes even farther and pours out his heart about how Estella made him feel. Poor lonely kid—he has no confidante but Joe, who doesn't understand what he's talking about.

But Joe's advice to Pip zooms in on the heart of the matter: "Lies is lies." He gets muddled, though, which gives Pip room to become skeptical. So when Joe's advice—that Pip should stick to his own kind—gets hard to take, Pip pulls back, and looks around critically, taking Estella's perspective. The final sentence foreshadows how inextricably Pip is bound to Miss Havisham's world already.

In chapter 10 Dickens attacks Mrs. Wopsle's school in more detail than in chapter 7; the tone has changed to harsher satire. Now Pip is more critical of his surroundings, and, anxious to get ahead, he's impatient with anything that holds him back. Biddy, who seemed merely a sloppy child before, now appears to be the only person with any sense in the place. Pip's arrangement to get extra lessons from her sets him apart from the other boys, who avoid education like the plague.

When Pip stops by the local pub to pick up Joe, his attention is caught by a stranger. Though the man appears harmless, talking about mundane things like turnips, he seems to threaten Pip. His one-eyed glance looks like he's aiming a gun, and he rubs his leg meaningfully (recalling the convict's leg-iron). The stranger's talk keeps linking back to Pip's meeting with the convict. For the crowning touch, the stranger nonchalantly stirs his drink with the same file Pip stole.

Amid the adults in the pub, only Pip understands what the stranger is referring to. But when the stranger gives him a shilling wrapped up in paper—two one-pound notes—Pip doesn't understand why. He doesn't even wonder about it, but allows Mrs. Joe to take the money and set it aside. He's haunted again, however, by the memory of the convict.

CHAPTER 11

On his second visit to Miss Havisham, Pip has a series of illogical encounters; but, almost in a trance, he accepts everything quietly. Estella off-handedly leads him first into a back room with a small group of other people. Pip's moral sense at once picks up that these people are toadies and humbugs (a type we've met in Pumblechook). Their conversation baffles Pip, the outsider, as they discuss people he doesn't know and pick apart social customs unfamiliar to a working-class boy. Nothing explains why Pip is taken there, then led away by Estella while they continue to wait.

On the unlit stairs, Pip next meets a large dark man who examines him sharply, passes pessimistic judgment on him, and pushes past. Note his characteristics; he'll reappear.

Upstairs, Pip is given a new job—to walk Miss Havisham slowly around the weird dining room, where a bridal feast rots on the table. Again, Miss Havisham has an ulterior motive; she knows his presence will gall her relatives (the toadies) when they're brought upstairs. The "nervous invalid" Camilla pours out lavish, false protests of love for Miss Havisham, and walnut-faced Sarah throws in her back-stabbing comments. What an unpleasant crew! But Miss Havisham sees through them; she flies into a passion, denounces them as parasites, and sends them away. Afterwards, she seems human for a moment, sadly telling Pip that it's her birthday. She quickly turns this, however, into a melodramatic speech, in which she fervidly pictures herself rotting towards death. Pip is wordless, so caught by her spell that he feels as though he's beginning to decay, too.

After another insult session over cards with Estella,

Pip goes out to the garden, where still another stranger pops out of nowhere—the pale young gentleman. His immediate invitation to come and fight astonishes Pip, but, without a question, Pip obeys. The pale young gentleman has a definite set of boxing conventions; Pip follows his lead dimly. Like Estella, this boy has a confident way of carrying himself that intimidates—and impresses—insecure Pip. Though the other boy's covered with ink blots (he's struggling with education, just as Pip is) and he's at a gawky age, he is a "gentleman" to Pip, a superior being. Pip is therefore astounded when his clumsy blows knock the boy flat. Yet Pip doesn't enjoy this victory; instead, he's awed by the other boy's game spirit. Pip is detached from his fighting, embarrassed by it as proof of his animal nature (overlooking the fact that the other boy started the fight). We really see Pip's inferiority complex here.

One more unaccountable event: Estella, flushed and eager, lets Pip kiss her cheek as he's going out the door. Presumably, she watched the fight from a hiding place, and felt the winner deserved a prize. But the fight wasn't anything to do with her—or was it? At any rate, it has excited her. Pip takes the kiss, gratefully; but he at once ruins his own pleasure by dwelling on the condescending spirit in which it was offered. Pip returns, dazed by all these odd events, through a black night to the light of Joe's forge.

CHAPTERS 12 & 13

Pip's strong sense of guilt and his vivid imagination torment him for days, as he wonders how he'll be punished for beating up the pale young gentleman. When he returns to Miss Havisham's, however, the incident isn't even mentioned, fitting in with the illogical pace of events at Satis House.

For the next eight to ten months, Pip becomes a regular at Miss Havisham's, going there every other day to push her around her rooms in a wheel chair. Though this is a relatively short span of time, it comes at a stage in Pip's life—he's probably about thirteen—when he's changing rapidly every day. At this vulnerable age, he's open to new influences. It's always been planned for Pip to become Joe's apprentice when he reaches the proper age (usually fourteen), but now, infected by what he has heard from his sister and Pumblechook, he hopes Miss Havisham will change all that. When Miss Havisham asks him perfectly normal questions about his future plans, he replies vaguely. Passively, shyly, he's waiting for an offer. He's also passive around Estella. She continues to be contrary and cold, but Pip doesn't ask himself why she treats him this way. He pretends not to overhear Miss Havisham whispering to her, "Break their hearts!" While Pip takes this all very seriously, Dickens wants to make us see how grotesque it is, so he throws in a glimpse of Pip, Miss Havisham, and Estella singing Joe's song from the forge, a lugubrious chant that's comically, weirdly, out of place.

Pip's growing more thin-skinned and sensitive, too. He stops confiding in Joe, choosing Biddy instead—hoping she won't give him the kind of honest tough advice Joe does. Pip also can't bear to hear Pumblechook and Mrs. Joe discuss his future—even though (or perhaps because) they echo Pip's own hopes.

Finally, Miss Havisham offers to help Pip with his apprenticeship papers ("articles"). Notice that in this conversation, Pip doesn't quote what he says, as if he's too upset to hear himself speak. When he brings this news home, Mrs. Joe works off her anxiety by scrubbing Pip and Joe out of the house. It's a familiar comic scene, and yet now it doesn't seem so funny. For once, even Mrs. Joe is in tune with Pip's worry.

All dressed up, the Gargerys look ludicrous—to Pip's mortified eyes—when they go to town the next day. Luckily, Mrs. Joe wasn't invited to Satis House, so she stays at Pumblechook's, but Joe is bad enough. He's completely out of his element at Satis House, fiddling with his hat in his hands, walking on the tips of his toes. Pip, who's used to this weird house by now, doesn't describe it again; if Joe looks foolish, we must recall what there is around there to amaze him. Joe's dialect comes out unusually strong, and he addresses himself to Pip as though he can't face Miss Havisham. Miss Havisham doesn't seem to mind— she can see how good Joe is—but Estella hangs over the back of her chair, laughing silently at Pip. He's embarrassed for Joe, and embarrassed of Joe, both at the same time. Miss Havisham acts quite sane, asking considerate questions and presenting Pip with a nice little sum of money; Joe is the one who looks crazy here. This reflects Pip's own sympathies at the moment.

That painful scene is followed by simpler comedy, when Joe teasingly hands over Pip's present to Mrs. Joe. For all her plotting, she's perfectly content with the twenty-five pounds, but Pip isn't. Feeling bitter and disappointed, he focuses on how offensive Pumblechook is, and he viciously satirizes the Justices in the Town Hall who certify the apprenticeship. Pip's sour mood continues as the family goes out to celebrate; feeling so alienated, he can't dramatize the lively scene, he can only describe it with loathing. He ends the chapter on a stubborn, snotty, resentful note—underlaid with pain and despair.

CHAPTERS 14 & 15

The direct, honest, quiet tone with which Pip
begins this section shows a new attitude—grudging
surrender. He describes his previous, contented vision of home, only to show how shame replaced it.
He doesn't want to analyze why he feels this way; he
just accepts the grim, stifling finality of his lot in life.
Miserably, he hallucinates, seeing Estella's scornful
face peering in at the forge, and the strains of their
song, "Old Clem," mock him.

But Pip never breathes a word of his discontent to
Joe. It's typical of Pip to hide his emotions, but here he
does it for kind reasons. He won't take credit for this,
however, placing all the emphasis instead upon Joe's
sterling qualities. Desperately pursuing education
himself, he takes Joe out to the Battery on a Sunday to
teach him to read, but he says he only wanted to raise
Joe so he wouldn't be so embarrassing. Pip focuses on
the worst sides of his own motives, and therefore he
can't appreciate that he is, in fact, being good.

Whereas Joe enjoys these Sundays, restless Pip
only notices the moving things—sails, clouds, sunlight—and longs for Satis House. He tries to convince
Joe that he owes Miss Havisham a visit, but Joe gives
some more of his hard-to-take advice—stay away. As
usual, Joe rambles on and dilutes his good sense with
nonsense, so Pip stops taking him seriously and
decides to do what he wants to do anyway.

Now that he's aware of the common, ugly elements
of his life, it's appropriate that Pip introduces the
forge's day-laborer, Dolge Orlick. Pip makes no bones
about hating Orlick. Orlick has always been resentful,
malicious, and hostile to Pip. To us, his slouching
surly manner shows out-and-out badness, next to

which Pip looks upright, no matter how bad he thinks he is. When Mrs. Joe objects to Joe giving Orlick a holiday, Orlick almost gleefully pitches into an argument with her. Joe tries to ward it off, but they won't even hear him (notice the parentheses around his speeches). They both relish the fight, and Mrs. Joe hams it up, calling on Joe to defend her honor. Against his kind nature, Joe responds. He appears strong and manly here, taking care of Orlick in no time, while Mrs. Joe faints from excitement. (Compare this fight to Pip's with the pale young gentleman).

Right after this brawl, Pip returns to Miss Havisham's to find it unchanged—except in the most important respect: Sarah Pocket answers the door because Estella has gone abroad, farther from Pip than ever. Feeling let down, Pip wanders home, so listless that Wopsle can even talk him into an evening at Pumblechook's.

NOTE: The play they're reading is *George Barnwell*, an 18th-century play by George Lillo about a London apprentice who fell in love with a wicked girl who made him kill his uncle for money. Pip doesn't notice it, but it's apt that he play this character.

Going home later, Pip and Wopsle meet Orlick, a menacing figure drifting in the shadows. Pip's old secret is evoked by the distant firing of the prison ship's guns. Immediately afterwards, Pip learns that somebody—convicts, it's suspected—broke into their house and attacked Mrs. Joe. Though she'll live, her well-meaning but wrong-minded energy has been unnaturally snuffed out.

CHAPTERS 16 & 17

Typically, Pip at first feels guilty for Mrs. Joe's attack. He realizes this is silly the next day, but as clues are revealed, Pip discovers a tangible cause for guilt. Whoever struck Mrs. Joe used a filed-apart leg-iron, which Pip knows came from his convict (that incident refuses to die). Pip, on sheer hunch, suspects either the one-eyed stranger from the pub, or Orlick. But he has no proof, and the London detectives from Bow Street are complete incompetents, so the mystery goes unsolved. Violence seems to have sprung irrationally out of nowhere, and still roams wild.

Brain damage has left Mrs. Joe an invalid. This once-forbidding household grows quiet, and then a gentler influence moves in as Biddy comes to nurse Mrs. Joe. This helps to comfort Joe who, we notice with respect, genuinely mourns his wife's accident. It's particularly galling that the police strongly suspect he did it.

The mystery is somewhat cleared up when Mrs. Joe takes an intense interest in Orlick. (She's got a mental block on his name, but she describes him on her writing slate with a T, standing for his hammer—a tool of violence, and a tool of the devil.) Her ingratiating manner towards him not only shows how much she has changed, but also suggests she's afraid of him—that he was her attacker. Pip never draws this conclusion, however. Perhaps he doesn't want to know evil, or perhaps he's too passive to do anything about it.

Pip begins to settle into this life. When he visits Miss Havisham, he sees how dull and gloomy the house is, now that Estella isn't there. Pip's still under her influence, but at the same time he's noticing Biddy—slowly and unconsciously—not instantly, as he fell for Estella.

NOTE: Pip and Biddy If you judge Pip harshly, you'll see he's condescendingly admiring Biddy, and rejecting his feelings for her. If you judge him kindly, you'll see that he's simply unaware of how quiet affection can ripen into real love (as opposed to infatuation).

Pip's Sunday walk with Biddy resembles the Sundays with Joe, except that Biddy is too honest to let things stay peaceful. Pip, confiding his ambitions to Biddy, blurts out his secret love for Estella. Why? Because he feels attracted to Biddy, he may be trying to share his most intense feelings with her; or he may be trying to protect himself against getting involved with her. Either way, since he knows how she feels about him, he's being thoughtlessly cruel. You'll have to imagine her reactions to this conversation—Pip can't afford to record them honestly. Note two things: Biddy gives hard advice, just as Joe would; and she doesn't say things she could to draw Pip back, because she won't lie. It's an agonizing, realistic scene of two souls never quite linking up, but coming so close. You may dislike Pip here, but you may also feel sorry for him. When he describes love as "That wonderful inconsistency into which the best and wisest of men fall every day," it's hard to blame him for this obstinate madness.

However, when Orlick appears to be paying Biddy attention, Pip feels jealous; his feelings for Biddy are still there. Orlick's continual presence makes Pip's life seem grim. Orlick's a real problem, but Pip doesn't deal with him; he's too uncertain of what world he wants to live in. And as the section ends, there's a hint that Pip's indecision will be resolved in a surprising way.

CHAPTER 18

Pip seems contented, spending a cheery evening at the pub, part of the crowd listening to Wopsle read a report of a murder trial. Wopsle now seems a friend, not an annoying adult; the description of his reading is not satirical but entertaining (Dickens appreciated actors). The warm comic scene, however, is chilled when a stranger speaks up. He punctures Wopsle's effect by grilling the audience on legal interpretations of the case. This is the second stranger who has asked for Pip at the Three Jolly Bargemen; the first brought him a file from the convict. But this one is different; Pip recognizes him from Miss Havisham's house (chapter 11).

The stranger impresses everyone with his air of authority; Joe even opens the parlor when they go home to talk in private. The lawyer, Jaggers, explains his business precisely, almost too methodically. In spite of his dry legal language, the facts that emerge are fantastic. Pip is going to get a fortune someday; his education for this will begin now. Pip wants social status more than wealth and, magically, becoming a gentleman is an essential part of his "great expectations." Not only has Pip's dream come true, it has come true on strange terms, as in a fairy-tale: Pip must not ask who his benefactor is.

NOTE: Pip's Response to His Good Fortune Why doesn't Pip object to this secret? Maybe he doesn't want to look a gift horse in the mouth; it's also his nature not to pry into mysteries. But basically he has already guessed that his patron is Miss Havisham. Look at the evidence. He met Jaggers first at Satis House; his tutor is going to be Miss Havisham's cousin; Mrs. Joe and Pumblechook always said she'd make him rich.

Pip is so stunned and overjoyed that he can't hear himself speaking, and so we don't get an exact quote of what he says. He says little, in his shy, tightly-controlled way. Joe's reaction is different. He realizes tht he's losing his closest friend, and he's insulted, almost belligerent, when businesslike Jaggers keeps offering him money. Joe accepted the apprentice premium from Miss Havisham—Pip earned that—but this money is more like a bribe, and Joe won't touch it. Crazy Miss Havisham saw the good in Joe, but worldly Jaggers just thinks he's a sentimental idiot. This may be more of a comment on the world's values than on Joe.

Already, Pip's fortune is making him unhappy. He resents Biddy and Joe's sadness, because, selfishly, he needs them to join in his joy. He gets defensive at their amazement, because he secretly feels unworthy inside. He can't share his news with other village people, fearing that their "coarse and common" reaction would degrade him. His shame of his surroundings intensifies, as his room, even the stars, seem humble and poor. Biddy challenges him on this bad attitude, but Pip ignores her warning and takes it as an insult, for which he must "forgive" her.

Pip thinks he's glad to be escaping his common life, until a wordless, homely scene makes him feel lost and lonely. Dickens handles it simply, as Pip, looking down from his window, spies Joe and Biddy comforting each other. Pip says he never again slept easy in his bed; but he forgets that he had been miserable there before. Money has changed his future, but Pip's restlessness came long before any fortune.

CHAPTER 19

Pip's conceited attitude is reflected in his elaborate language as he describes that next Sunday. In his new lofty status, he pities the villagers. He even remembers the convict without fear or remorse, as though he has finally risen above his shame over that association.

Taking a farewell tour of the marshes, Pip falls asleep (some readers say this symbolizes a moral lapse). He wakes to find Joe, looking like a comic dunce, joining him for one last talk. Joe misunderstands what Pip says to him about their changed relations. On one hand, this shows how stupid Joe can be, but on the other hand it emphasizes that what Pip's trying to express is off-base, morally—honest Joe can't comprehend it. Back home, Biddy immediately picks up on Pip's faulty reasoning, and calls him to task for not realizing that it insults Joe to talk of changing him. Pip isn't on Biddy's wavelength, though; he assumes she's being difficult because she's jealous. Pip the narrator tells us that Pip the character speaks in a "virtuous and superior tone", implicitly criticizing him.

Pip imagines that he should be treated differently now. Biddy and Joe won't play that game, but other people do. Trabb, the tailor, falls all over himself to please Pip as soon as he learns Pip's a gentleman; Pip eats it up, and enjoys seeing Trabb's audacious servant boy put in his place. Other tradesmen in town pander to Pip too. The supreme fawner is, as you'd expect, Pumblechook. He treats Pip to dinner, sparing no expense. Anxious to play up to Pip, he speaks of Joe as a simpleton and criticizes Mrs. Joe, his old ally, for her temper, but recalls what good friends he and Pip have always been.

NOTE: Pip Loses His Moral Bearings It's annoying to see Pumblechook echoing, in exaggerated form, Pip's opinion of other people; this makes us feel Pip has gone wrong. To let himself get drunk with Pumblechook is the most degrading thing Pip could do; again he falls asleep, literally and morally.

Pip eagerly prepares to leave for London. (Notice he's ready far in advance. Haven't you ever done this, before an exciting trip?) But Pip's dissatisfied with the way he looks in his new clothes, his old self-consciousness aggravated by a new self-importance. Full of himself, he makes his farewell visit to Miss Havisham. The way she gloats and knows everything already from Jaggers, makes him more sure than ever that she's his patron, so he reads a hidden message in everything she says. He looks ridiculous kneeling to kiss her hand, but after all, it's all he can do to show his gratitude.

Pip looks ridiculous, too, the last night at home when he sits in his fancy clothes by the fire with Joe and Biddy, but this is less embarrassing because the scene shows Pip's good side, which is really sad to leave them. He knows it's selfish not to let Joe walk him to the coach, and he almost tells Joe he can come—but not quite. This conflict, and his reluctance to go downstairs the final morning, show that he hasn't lost all moral bearings. When Biddy and Joe throw shoes after him, he's both embarrassed and touched by the homely custom. He describes the village in a simple, gentle language as he is leaving, and tears of strong emotion overtake him, cleansing his soul. He even thinks about going back and making a second, better farewell, but indecision robs him of chance. Restless and insecure as ever, Pip forgets the future he longed for so intensely. He can only look back, regretting his own behavior, as the coach drags him toward a new life.

PART II

CHAPTERS 20 & 21

Part II—the second stage of Pip's expectations—whirls us into a new atmosphere. In these days before trains, not to mention cars or planes, people didn't travel far from home; though it's only five hours away, London would have been like another planet to a village boy. Pip has always heard of it in such glowing terms that he's surprised to see how crowded, dirty, and rundown it is. Dickens, who knew London well, chooses specific neighborhoods to show us, stinking Smithfield and morbid Newgate Prison. One more element of Pip's dream-come-true is a letdown.

In this immense city, Jaggers is an important person. The coachman who takes Pip to the office is pretty savvy (a 19th-century version of a New York cabbie), yet even he is in awe of Jaggers. But Jaggers' office isn't grand; it's a dismal, small room, full of strange objects—weapons, suspicious boxes, and two ugly plaster busts—with a greasy spot on the wall evoking a picture of dirty, cringing clients. Unsavory types huddle in the courtyard, and Jaggers' name is muttered on all sides, almost like a charm. When he walks in, he's practically mobbed. His brief, cautious conversations with the clients are cryptic; we can only guess what illegal affairs they involve. Jaggers seems unwilling to touch these people, and, talking to one of them, Mike, he furiously avoids hearing any incriminating phrase. But Pip refers to Jaggers as "my guardian"; so we can't ignore how closely Pip is tied to him.

Pip doesn't seem conscious of the bad association, but it spreads a shadow over how we see Pip's new station in life.

Wemmick, Jagger's chief clerk, at first seems callous and cynical, carelessly advising Pip to visit filthy Smithfield, elbowing Mike during his interrogation, shoving clients out of his path. He is described as having a dry, wood-like, dinted face, glittering eyes, and a wide slot of a mouth. He's a jaded Londoner, making Pip seem like a naive country boy. Yet this contrast makes Pip look good. When he offers to shake hands with Wemmick, he shows a friendliness and trust that's often lost in the big city. But we wonder what could happen to Pip, if he stays in London.

NOTE: On Dicken's Style In the description of Barnard's Inn, we can see the hallmarks of Dickens' consciously "artistic" style. Note the piled-up repetitions of "dismal" or "rot," the clutter of sharply-observed details, and the increasingly fantastic tone. The prose even falls into iambic pentameter, taking on the rhythms of poetry.

In this dirty, unwelcoming place, Herbert Pocket, Pip's host, turns out to be a delightful young fellow, talking a mile a minute, his arms full of food and his face full of laughter. He too recognizes the grime and mess. At last, after a day of new experiences, Pip finds a congenial spirit; what's more, he's a familiar figure from home—none other than the pale young gentleman Pip fought at Miss Havisham's.

NOTE: The Role of Coincidence Many readers object to coincidences like this in Dickens' novels. Dickens pointed out that things like this constantly happen in real life. At this point, too, Pip doesn't think meeting Herbert is a coincidence; anything that links him with Miss Havisham just confirms his suspicion that she's his patron. But coincidence does play a large part in this book, tying together the intricate pattern of subplots. As you read, consider how these coincidences also fit into Dickens' view of life.

CHAPTER 22

Pip's new life gets off the ground now, as he and Herbert enjoy a huge, sloppy feast, on their own in the big city. Herbert Pocket's healthy ego contrasts to Pip's insecurity. Herbert believes he won their long-ago fight; he isn't bothered by his failure to become Miss Havisham's heir; he isn't interested in Estella's cruel games. In comparison, Pip holds back, reluctant to correct Herbert or to confide his own feelings, even though he likes Herbert a lot. (Pip admires Herbert's "frank and easy way," something he himself lacks.) Pip briefly tells his story to Herbert; he adds, in painfully polite tones, that he'd like Herbert's help in learning to be a gentleman. Some readers feel Pip is a snob, trying too hard to impress Herbert. Others see that he's shy, and has a hard time opening up to anybody, especially someone he looks up to like Herbert.

Herbert gives Pip a new nickname—Handel. As they talk, Herbert tactfully corrects Pip's table manners. This is the first time we've seen Pip's lower-class manners; Pip's either too aware of himself still—or too embarrassed—to tell us about them himself.

Herbert tells Pip Miss Havisham's weird history—of her worthless half-brother, the scheming suitor, Matthew Pocket's argument with her, the aborted wedding, and her violent reaction. This is the first time Pip has heard her story explained; perhaps he was too fascinated by her bizarre lifestyle to question it before, or perhaps his shyness kept him from prying. Even Herbert doesn't know all the details, whether the brother and suitor were in cahoots or what happened to them after; he doesn't know any more about Estella, either. Elements of mystery persist.

The mystery of Pip's benefactor is skirted, but Herbert seems to understand, without saying so aloud, that it's Miss Havisham. Herbert's agreement on this—and his sense that marrying Estella is part of the deal—adds more weight to Pip's belief. In contrast to Pip's mysterious but grand expectations, we hear Herbert's own dreams for his future as a shipping merchant. These seem like normal fantasies, and he's cheerful and optimistic about them; he's also working hard towards them. He's on a logical career track, whereas Pip's jump up in class has been extraordinary.

Pip feels as though years lie between him and the old village. Looking back, he feels guilty about how he treated Joe and Biddy. The next morning, he visits the Royal Exchange (" 'Change"), headquarters of the shipping insurance companies. Dickens gives us here another of his capsule satires of London (Dickens didn't have much sympathy for commercial types.) We have a sense that Pip hasn't moved up into a better world, only into a different one. This feeling grows as we visit the chaotic Pocket household that afternoon. Compare careless Mrs. Pocket to tyrannical Mrs. Joe. The Pocket children's "tumbling up" childhood seems just as inadequate as Pip's upbringing "by hand."

CHAPTERS 23 & 24

Now that Pip's in London, he has to learn its social customs. Dickens therefore moves from his former tragedy-comedy blend into chapters of social satire.

At the Pockets', the social order is upside down. Both of the grownup Pockets were bred to higher expectations than they've reached: Mrs. Pocket, obsessed with titles, has only a flimsy claim to aristocratic pretensions; Mr. Pocket has a top-notch education, but it has gotten him nowhere. His authority over his pupils is uncertain, too. The absent-minded teacher looks young in spite of his gray hair; his student Drummle is the opposite, an old-looking young man. The other pupil, Startop, seems too delicate to handle so much learning. The household is really run by the servants, not the masters. The kitchen serves better food than the dining room upstairs, and the nurse can swat the baby if she pleases; like the tradesmen who fawned on Pip, these servants consider the moneyed classes to be fair prey. Dickens had a reputation as a radical, but he seems to fear this undermining of the social order.

Pip, who has to concentrate on his table manners, quietly observes the dinner party. The snakelike neighbor Mrs. Coiler—a total caricature—and Drummle, the lumpish baronet-to-be, play up to Mrs. Pocket's snobbery. All this makes Herbert uncomfortable. (Herbert is a good index of how Dickens expects us to react, throughout the novel.) When the children come in, Dickens describes them as interchangeable objects, reflecting how little attention anyone pays them. The baby's an "it," always upside down or doubling over. At the same time, the little Pockets act like miniature adults, dutifully watching out for each other, patiently waiting to be cared for. Again, the natural order is overturned. This is comedy, but in an exaggerated, almost manic mood. Pip, who's still getting his bearings, does not comment on it, but Dickens' tone suggests that we should be critical.

This impractical domestic scene contrasts to the tough business environment of Jaggers' office, where Pip goes soon to arrange for sharing rooms with Herbert. Jaggers grills Pip on how much money he wants (almost as Pumblechook did—except that Jaggers is harshly negotiating real sums of money). Wemmick, Jaggers' hard but lively clerk, openly admires the lawyer's bullying manner and inscrutable skills. Everyone here seems to have been taken over and warped by his work. Jaggers' other clerks—on display, almost like animals in a little zoo—are nothing but grotesque caricatures. Wemmick shows off the plaster busts in Jaggers' office with affection; we gather, however, that these were a pretty grisly pair of clients, who were cast in plaster after having been hanged. Wemmick's imaginative nature seems to have taken off in perverse directions. His own particular obsession is money—or, rather, "portable property" (people in Jaggers' world always have a precise legalistic term for everything). Wemmick is somehow an appealing person, however; he invites Pip to come to his house for dinner sometime, and Pip accepts.

The final paragraph gives us Jaggers, like a powerful wizard, in control of the courtroom. This scene is impressionistic, not realistic; we see faces and figures in confusing glimpses, we don't catch the exact words that are spoken, the mood is exaggerated and intense. Jaggers is a force to be reckoned with here, but this isn't the kind of world Pip expected to be "lifted" into.

CHAPTERS 25 & 26

In these two chapters, we get an idea of Pip's widening social circle.

First, Pip describes his fellow students; Drummle he finds thoroughly unpleasant, while Startop is weak but inoffensive. Both have had inadequate parents and neglected educations. There's an echo of Orlick in the way Drummle slouches and hides in the shadows. He's the only real aristocrat we meet in this book; this doesn't make the upper classes come off very well.

Pip describes these two, and the Pocket cousins, in hard clear-sighted terms. He's just as hard on himself, admitting he's a spendthrift, and refusing to take credit for doing well at his studies (just as he wouldn't take credit for doing well at the forge). Pip is still dissatisfied, quicker to note his own faults than anyone else's. Yet he responds to the good in Herbert, Matthew Pocket, and Wemmick. Pip reminds Wemmick of his dinner invitation, showing he wants to make friends.

Wemmick at first confirms our view of him, as he hard-headedly previews the menu. Yet by the time Pip and Wemmick reach his home, the clerk's values have turned inside out. His nutty little gothic cottage, with all its daily rituals, is totally inefficient—and that's the glory of it. The lake is purely ornamental, the garden paths twist around for no reason, and Wemmick has spent years creating all this. Wemmick's home life is so different from his office life, he draws a sharp division between them. He protects his home by a moat and battlements from the threatening world outside. He even seems prepared for a siege, with his own garden and livestock. Some readers think he's smart to escape from Jaggers' business.

Others, however, think he lacks the integrity to live a consistent life. As you read, watch how the halves of his life fit together.

Pip enjoys his evening at Wemmick's, and doesn't complain about the dry-rot taste of the dinner or the cramped bedroom he sleeps in. Though the cottage is stuffed with curiosities, everything is neatly in place, including the most important element—family affection. Wemmick and his "Aged Parent" are one of the book's few examples of a loving parent and child.

Jaggers' house, which Pip visits next, is quite different. Like Wemmick, Jaggers tries to get rid of the office's stain; he furiously washes himself at the end of the day. But Jaggers' mind doesn't change. His house is full of law books and he often brings work home. His home, like his personality, is dark, heavy, repressed, morbid; the wall carvings even look like nooses. Wemmick pours energy into making his home grow, but Jaggers uses his energy to keep everything under rigid control. He won't give out his address, but leads Pip and his friends there. At dinner he himself serves everyone, afterwards dropping their dirty dishes fastidiously into a basket.

The atmosphere drifts into melodrama. Jaggers' housekeeper, with her streaming hair and haunted face, is like a tragic heroine, Lady Macbeth. When Jaggers shows off her powerful wrists, it's a display of his own strength, that he can imprison such a woman. She is the opposite of Wemmick's weak, helpless, but beloved Aged Parent.

Jaggers casts an antisocial mood around him. Though Pip lists several delicious dishes, he doesn't really enjoy the meal. All the guests show off their worst sides, and an ugly argument arises between Drummle and Pip. At Wemmick's, the gun was shot at nine o'clock for fun, not to mark time; at Jaggers', the host's pocketwatch is pulled out strictly at 9:30 and guests are sent home. After they leave, Jaggers scrubs up again, as though his guests disgust him as much as his clients do. When Pip returns, Jaggers warns him to avoid Drummle, though Jaggers likes him; we sense Jaggers is drawn to the evil side of human nature.

CHAPTERS 27 & 28

How have these new experiences affected Pip? When Joe Gargery comes to visit, we can measure the change in Pip.

Now we realize how Pip has neglected Joe and Biddy. Joe's letter to Pip (written by Biddy) is strained and polite; in her private P.S., Biddy sounds wary of Pip's new attitudes. And Pip does admit to mixed feelings towards Joe's visit. Pip's sensitivity seems to be two-edged. He's afraid of others (especially despicable Drummle and his own cocky servant boy) looking down on him because of Joe. But he also seems afraid that Joe will disapprove of his extravagant furnishings and unnecessary servant.

Pip sits in his room, nerves on edge, listening to Joe coming upstairs with maddening slowness. Joe bursts in with glowing good humor at first, but something begins to confuse him; as before with Miss Havisham, he clings to his hat brim and his dialect sounds strong. He starts to talk in circles, and he formally calls Pip "sir." Pip irritably watches Joe fiddling with his hat, which constantly falls off the mantle; he wonders why Joe wears those uncomfortable collars and why his manners are so bad. (Haven't you done this in a stressful situation—focusing on irrelevant details?) Yet Pip himself is to blame for making Joe ill at ease.

When he criticizes Joe's formality, Joe's wordless glance in reply reminds us suddenly of his natural dignity. Joe delivers a message from Miss Havisham: Estella is home and wishes to see Pip. Pip suddenly feels grateful to Joe (and embarrassed that he needs a reason to feel grateful). He tries to treat Joe better, but with simple eloquence Joe backs out of Pip's new life, where he knows he doesn't belong. Pip feels moved, but, just like the morning he left home, he runs after Joe too late. Why do you think Pip treats Joe like this? (How would you behave in similar circumstances?) Some readers claim Pip is being a snob. Others say he's still insecure in his new social position.

Joe, Biddy, Miss Havisham, and Estella have now been woven back into the plot; in the next chapter the persistent memory of the convict returns, too. Preparing to go home, Pip's at a weak moment, selfishly concerned about what kind of impression he will make. Then when he gets to the coach, he learns he has to ride with a pair of convicts—and one of them is the man with the file who brought Pip money at the pub. Perhaps because he's a snob—or because he's becoming socially refined—Pip is disgusted by their crude manners, though he also shows us how pitiful they are. The atmosphere's cold and rainy (this seems to be typical "convict weather"). Forced to listen to the convicts' conversation, Pip learns that the one-eyed convict brought him that money long ago from "his" convict. The one-eyed man would never recognize Pip now, but Pip's so terrified by this connection that he jumps off the coach early and walks the rest of the way.

When he gets to the hotel in town Pip discovers he has another "patron"—Pumblechook, who has been telling everyone that he's responsible for Pip's rise.

Pumblechook isn't as shameful a patron as the convict, but he's more galling, because his motives are so obvious and selfish.

CHAPTER 29

Returning to Miss Havisham's, Pip sees it all in fairy-tale terms: he is the Knight, Estella is the Princess, and Satis House is an enchanted castle to be freed from its spell. This romantic view exists easily alongside his rational knowledge that Estella's not perfect. Dickens is working out his definition of love—an emotion that is so powerful and perverse that it can survive any attacks from mere reality.

In this fairy-tale house, figures from Pip's past magically appear. The first is Orlick, who's now the porter, like a sullen dragon guarding the gate. Sarah Pocket pops up next, a green-and-yellow gremlin. When he finally reaches Miss Havisham's room, Pip sees an elegant lady—a stranger, he thinks, until he sees her eyes and knows it's Estella.

Pip may have changed a lot, but Estella has changed even more, putting more distance than ever between her and Pip. All of his self-confidence wilts before this beauty. Estella has developed a woman's languid, detached manner to lure men on, as opposed to her girlish, spiteful manner. Walking in the garden with Pip, she alternately does and doesn't remember the incidents etched so deeply in his memory, as though she's teasing him. Carelessly, she tells him that she has no heart—a bold, shocking statement such as Miss Havisham likes to make. But something about Estella reminds Pip of somebody else—not Miss Havisham—he can't place it. If you've ever had this kind of *déjà vu* sensation, you can imagine how it's going to nag Pip until he places it.

Back inside, Miss Havisham is unchanged and grotesque. She feeds ravenously on Pip's admiration of Estella, repeating to him fiercely "Love her," working herself into a violent fit. As Pip calms her, a scent alerts him to another familiar presence: Jaggers. Even Miss Havisham acts afraid of Jaggers, who, under the influence of this household, seems an exaggerated version of himself, more cynical and insinuating. He questions Pip accusingly about Estella and Miss Havisham, and torments Sarah Pocket by referring to Pip's expectations. Estella seems fascinated by him, maybe because he never looks at her (men usually don't treat her that way).

The house Pip thought of as a fairy-tale is turning into a nightmare. Sarah Pocket is pulling out her hair in the next room, Miss Havisham is strewing jewels all over Estella, and the playing cards even seem to be coming alive to Pip. The effect is heightened since it is viewed through Pip's seething emotions. He blames Jaggers' cold presence for crushing his passionate feelings, yet Pip himself is penning up all his passion. His love twists feverishly in his mind: he longs to have Estella; then he remembers that she is going to marry him; then he finds that's not enough, he wants her love, too. In spite of what she has said about having no heart, he persists in believing his own fairy tale about her: that she's a sleeping beauty and he will awaken her.

Pip has been feeling guilty about not visiting Joe, but Satis House, which always brings out the worst in him, makes him feel ashamed of Joe again. Pip the narrator judges his young self sternly, pointing out how weak his good intentions were in the face of selfish love. Do you think Dickens blames Pip? Your answer will depend on which you think Dickens rates more highly—loyalty or love.

CHAPTERS 30 & 31

If we felt sorry for Pip at Miss Havisham's, his behavior the next morning strains our sympathy. First he pompously tells Jaggers that Orlick is unsuitable to work at Satis House; next, like a coward he circles miles to avoid Pumblechook. He's pleased, however, by the flattery of the tradesmen he meets. It's fitting that Trabb's boy should parade down the street behind Pip, outrageously imitating his haughty airs. As Dickens describes this wonderful play-acting, we're more in tune with Trabb's boy—lively, agile, and a shrewd observer—than with Pip. Of course Pip's mortified—wouldn't you be?—but listen to his prissy, offended reaction. This is exactly the attitude Trabb's boy is mocking.

In this parody, we see how others see Pip—and add this to our opinion of him. Pip's conversation with Herbert back in London is more realistic, but it still shows him in a harsh light. Pip dramatically confesses to Herbert that he loves Estella, only to find that Herbert has seen through him long ago. Herbert is supportive, and never mentions his opinion of Estella (remember what he said about her in chapter 22?). He tries to buck up Pip's spirits by telling him what a great guy he is.

NOTE: Mark Herbert's Sketch of Pip: "a good fellow, with impetuosity and hesitation, boldness and diffidence, action and dreaming, curiously mixed in him." Do you think this is a fair summary of Pip? Herbert should be a good judge, but we also know Pip's inner nature, as Herbert does not. We must put all these views together to know Pip.

Even optimistic Herbert is skeptical about Pip's hopes to marry Estella. He makes Pip see that Jaggers has never mentioned marriage as part of Pip's expectations. Like Biddy in chapter 17, Herbert probes Pip's feelings, kindly and yet severely. Can Pip possibly give up on Estella? Pip doesn't answer, but a stubborn rush of memory and feeling besets him at the thought. As Herbert shrewdly says, Pip is a boy "whom nature and circumstances made so romantic"; realistic Herbert tries to make Pip see Estella as she is, but, as we know, Pip clings obstinately to Estella.

One more mark against Pip: whereas Pip's secret love was obvious, Herbert has been hiding a fiancée from Pip. Perhaps Pip is too wrapped up in his own life to notice those around him. Herbert's situation is the opposite of Pip's; he has Clara's heart, but not enough money to marry. (Dickens himself once was young, poor, and desperate to get married.)

To console themselves, the two young men go out to the theater. This chapter is a spell of broad satire, as Dickens describes Wopsle's performance of Hamlet. Dickens' method is to play dumb—reducing the stage illusions to bald, literal terms (the King and Queen are sitting "in two arm-chairs on a kitchen table", for instance). The audience isn't moved at all by this production—you know the mood, if you've ever sat in a crowded movie theater with an awful film going on. Pip and Herbert feel sorry for Wopsle but they can't help laughing; afterwards Pip invites Wopsle to dinner, trying to be considerate. This evening of comic relief can't raise Pip's spirits, however. Wopsle's Hamlet adds to our image of Pip, for Pip has lately been playing a Prince too—and Trabb's boy teased him for it as cruelly as this audience teased Wopsle.

CHAPTERS 32 & 33

A cold careless note from Estella, summoning Pip to meet her in London, throws him into a frenzy. Reaching the coach station hours early, he meets Wemmick and, to relieve the agony of waiting, goes with him to look at Newgate Prison.

The description of Wemmick tending the prisoners as a gardener tends his plants is ironic, for these "shoots" are destined to die soon. Now that we've seen Wemmick's personal life, we're taken aback to see him in his professional manner again. Though he's only an extension of Jaggers, Wemmick relishes his cruel power, callously using it to get "portable property" and to taunt these desperate creatures.

Afterwards, Pip feels dirty and unworthy; the criminal taint of the prison seems to fill his lungs and coat his clothes. For some reason, he remembers his childhood encounter with the convict; it too contaminates him. All of this clashes against his image of Estella, separate, pure, and perfect. But as she pulls up in the coach, notice that Pip doesn't feel joyful; instead, he's nagged by that resemblance which he still can't place.

This is the first time we've seen Estella on her own. Her imperious manner seems like a mechanical performance; she lets Pip wait on her but makes it clear she takes no responsibility for it. She ironically refers to their "instructions"; this thrills Pip, assuring him they're bound together; yet also reminding him that their connection has been forced on her. Pip, in his usual Estella-state of mingled excitement and misery, tries to make gallant little speeches to her. This simply amuses her, but she does come out of her shell briefly to reveal contempt for Miss Havisham's scheming relatives. For the first time, we glimpse how wretched her childhood was.

NOTE: On Estella How do you see Estella here? Some readers believe she's a victim, warped by her upbringing. Others say she knows what she's like, and she could be different if she weren't so resigned to it. She certainly could treat Pip better if she wanted to, but she isn't entirely to blame; he creates a good half of his misery himself (after all, Herbert wouldn't let this kind of treatment get to him).

Pip has built Estella up into a goddess. He shudders when they pass Newgate in their carriage; she, however, is curious about Newgate and about Jaggers, whom Pip considers beneath her. Just then, that ominous resemblance springs up again in a glare of gaslight. The house at Richmond where Estella's staying is like a moonlit mirage from another era. She's reabsorbed into that timeless fairy-tale world, so different from the world of Newgate and Jaggers. Pip returns heartsick to the Pockets' house, where there's no one sensible and sensitive enough to confide his troubles to.

CHAPTERS 34 & 35

Pip takes a hard, guilt-wracked look at the changes in his character. His money has led him only into a more miserable way of life. He regrets the way he has treated Joe and Biddy, and feels uneasy about the bad habits he has led Herbert into. Notice how Pip's money makes him the social leader; Herbert trails behind, too proud to accept a loan. How bad are Pip's habits? True, he overspends, probably drinks a little too much at parties; yet he doesn't seem to be womanizing or gambling. In spite of the prudish literary customs of the time, Dickens could have shown us a much more degenerate social life. Some readers think Dickens disapproves of Pip, but others think he's showing how hard Pip always is on himself.

It's interesting that Pip focuses on what's happening to Herbert. Maybe Dickens is saying we recognize changes in other people better than in ourselves; maybe he's saying that Pip could let himself go to ruin, but is too good-hearted to let it happen to a friend. Either way, it's Herbert we see, hungover at breakfast, depressed at midnight, listlessly hunting for his big opportunity at the Royal Exchange. It's Pip who brightly suggests they sit down and "look into their affairs."

NOTE: Dickens' Need for Order Dickens himself was obsessive about order; he couldn't start work without his paper, pens, and inkwells lined up neatly, so no doubt he sympathized with Pip and Herbert's urge to label, list, and categorize their bills. Nevertheless, their elaborate system is all form and no substance—they still don't pay the bills. Maybe Dickens knew how easy it is to substitute organization for action, and his scornful tone here criticizes himself as much as Pip.

In the middle of feeling pleased with himself, Pip is halted abruptly by the news of Mrs. Joe's death. He's surprised how much this affects him. He may seem a little morbid here, but it's a natural reaction, especially when you're a teenager, when you realize that people you know can die. The tone here is sobered by death, yet Dickens satirizes the trappings of the old-fashioned funeral—paid mourners at the house door, heavy black outfits for the bereaved family, a formal procession stage-directed by the undertaker. In contrast, he seems to respect the religious burial rite, but then Pumblechook crops up, an ingratiating pest. This jarring blend of the solemn and the ridiculous is perfect tragi-comedy.

Sorrow has softened Pip, and he tries to mend his relations with Joe and Biddy after the funeral. However, traces of condescension remain; he thinks he's doing a great thing by requesting his old room to please Joe. Grief has softened Biddy, too, and she describes Mrs. Joe's death to Pip in simple, moving language. Yet she's still wary of Pip's new intentions to visit them more often—and with good reason, we feel. Pip's stung by Biddy's little barbs, but he assumes an air of silent injured dignity (remember the stuffy way he handled Trabb's boy?), perhaps privately knowing she's right. The parting scene the next morning paints Joe and Biddy in a warm, picturesque light, and Pip seems honestly determined to visit more often. But the mists surrounding his departure—symbols of his cloudy moral sense—imply that he'll fail them again.

CHAPTERS 36 & 37

Certain birthdays are milestones: we look forward to becoming old enough to drive, to vote, or to drink. But Pip's twenty-first birthday holds special importance; he hopes to learn something definite about his "expectations."

Pip's interview with Jaggers blasts his hopes. Waiting for the lawyer to speak, Pip for some reason recalls how he felt when the convict perched him on the tombstone. Jaggers seems agitated too, staring at his boots, cross-examining Pip, tightly withholding information, and outlining Pip's finances in strict legal lan-

guage. He disclaims any responsibility for these arrangements, though he slips in that he thinks they're
"injudicious." Some readers think Jaggers is cynically
saying that Pip can't handle a yearly allowance of five
hundred pounds; others think Jaggers disapproves of
the whole affair, and he's warning Pip not to get hurt
by his expectations. Pip feels that Jaggers is annoyed
by the plan for him to marry Estella. Notice that Pip is
still convinced that Miss Havisham is his patron and
that Estella is meant for him; but he hoped things
would become official today.

Jaggers is apparently trying to do well by Pip. Perhaps he acts cold because he's afraid to show any
affection, or because he's so cynical. He asks to join
Pip's birthday dinner, yet he only ruins the evening
for Pip and Herbert. Jaggers symbolizes the harsh
adult world to Pip, so his manner makes Pip regret
being an adult now.

But notice the first thing Pip does as a responsible
adult: he uses his money to help a friend, Herbert.
Wemmick, when he's consulted at the office, says not
to do it, but Pip then goes to Walworth the next Sunday to flush out his personal views. Life at the Castle
is comic, exaggerated, and yet affectionate. Wemmick
reveals another emotional tie—to Miss Skiffins, his
cartoon-like girlfriend. Pip is tempted to poke fun at
her garish clothes and angular figure, but then he realizes that she treats the Aged Parent well—which is
the most important value at Walworth. (Pip too treats
the Aged Parent well.) Miss Skiffins and Wemmick
are comical lovers—note the playful battle of Wemmick's arm trying time and again to steal around her
waist. Between the wooden plaques tumbling open at
every arrival, and the lubrications of plentiful toast
and tea, Pip feels cozily at home here.

As Pip suspected, Wemmick's "Walworth advice" is the opposite of his office advice; Wemmick approves totally of Pip's scheme and throws himself into it with cleverness and energy, finding the merchant Clarriker who needs a young partner, getting papers signed secretly. Pip handles the matter delicately, so Herbert never guesses he has a "patron" and believes he has succeeded on his own merits. Pip shows a good heart here. But consider: Wemmick has Miss Skiffins, now Herbert can have Clara. Where will that leave Pip?

CHAPTER 38

It leaves him with Estella. This whole section is devoted to Estella at Richmond, where Pip plays the role of a sort of eunuch escort. He's free to hang around her, but he almost seems to be considered harmless, rather than the favored suitor. He watches her torture scores of other admirers, while all he gets is a rare word of pity. His tone is weary, dogged, exasperated. Even though he believes she is reserved for him alone, he feels too shy about this to press his own cause, and simply follows her with mute passive devotion.

When they go to visit Miss Havisham, she seems weirder and more witch-like than before, devouring Estella with her eyes, watching Pip's misery with glittering satisfaction. Pip tries to figure out why Miss Havisham hasn't announced Estella's engagement to him. It must be because she can make everybody suffer at once, by letting Estella go on flirting with everyone except him.

Pip sees the awful setting—the candlelit gloom, the spooky decayed props—with fresh eyes. As the privileged insider, he finally observes the private relationship between Miss Havisham and Estella, too, in the form of a bitter fight. Estella treats Miss Havisham as coldly as she treats everyone—and Miss Havisham is astounded. Estella responds calmly that Miss Havisham made her heartless and must accept the consequences. The language here is melodramatic, the scene almost like an intense little play (or, in our times, a soap opera). There are several possible interpretations of Estella's behavior here: 1) she really is an unfeeling monster; 2) she knows Miss Havisham's tricks, and has found the only way to manipulate her back; or 3) she feels cheated by her upbringing and wants to punish Miss Havisham for it. Miss Havisham appears to be the victim again, a lonely, slightly crazy old lady whose scheme of revenge backfired on her. In her own perverse fashion, she has loved Estella and pinned all her hopes on her. Her emotional reaction cries out for pity. In contrast, Estella is intellectual and hard-headed; she develops a metaphor, comparing sunlight—which is always shut out here—to love, which she has never been taught to feel.

It's hard for Pip to watch this, in love with Estella as he is. He escapes, depressed, into the starlight (remember, Estella's always symbolized by stars). That night, sleeping at Satis House, he sees Miss Havisham, first in his dreams, then in her restless nightly wanderings, a pale ghostly tragic figure; we feel sorry for her, not for Estella.

But Pip still persists in adoring Estella. At his dining club, Pip discovers, through a crude drinking boast, that Bentley Drummle has been paying court to Estella. This offends Pip down to the roots of his soul, and nearly leads to a ridiculous duel. Recall how Pip reacted when Orlick was hanging around Biddy in

Chapters 17 and 35; here again, Pip insists that his main feeling is horror that so pure a creature should be defiled. He's jealous, but he also simply can't stand to think of Estella with such a brute. (Again, Pip draws a sharp line between good and evil.) Drummle, on the other hand, doesn't worship Estella; he regards Estella as his prey and, spider-like, he waits patiently to catch her.

One night, Pip confronts Estella about Drummle, but she shrugs it off, so certain that she's the one in control, entrapping him. Estella then reminds Pip that he's the only beau she doesn't toy with. This is special treatment—but not the kind Pip wants. We can only guess at Estella's motives here. Does she really care for Pip? Is she being kind, protecting him from her cruel games? Or does she realize that he's already caught, and this is the best way to break his heart?

After Pip is finished describing his grinding heart-ache, the last paragraph sets the scene for a disaster to come. Referring to an Oriental novel, *Tales of the Genii* (which Dickens read as a child), Pip pictures fate as a slab of stone, falling to crush the hero. We await Pip's fate nervously.

CHAPTER 39

In the previous chapter we saw Pip uselessly trail-ing behind Estella at parties; now we learn that he spends his days reading. He blames this aimlessness on the fact that his "expectations" are still so vague. If you were Pip, you, too, would probably be restless to get things settled.

Now we close in on a dramatic scene. It's a dark and stormy night (the kind of weather in which this novel began). Pip is alone in the top rooms of an out-of-the-way building near the river. You can hear the slashing rain, smell the smoky chimney, see the lights outdoors flickering. Winds howl, and bells toll the late hour. Then—a footstep falls.

When Pip listened to Joe climb the stairs, in chapter 27, he was ashamed. This time he's afraid. Imagine this as a movie scene, shot down a stairwell: a man circling upwards, moving in and out of a patch of light, his face hidden in shadow then visible for a moment. He's described in sentence fragments, in separate, disconnected details. Pip absorbs the facts, but can't comprehend why this ragged old sailor stretches his arms towards him. We can't blame Pip for his brusque manner; how would you react to a dirty stranger on a late, stormy night? But Pip also acts superior: he resents the man, thinks he's crazy, shrinks from him. Dickens makes Pip squirm; he draws out the suspense. The stranger sits, looks Pip over. Pip is about to grab him when, flash! he recognizes him. In emotional surges of words, he recalls that terrifying figure—the convict.

At first Pip pulls away and tells him, in frosty polite language, to get lost. The man's hurt look makes Pip act more kindly. But when Pip tries to give him money, the convict dramatically burns it. (Remember how Joe reacted when offered money?) The man has a certain power, despite his rough clothes and lower-class accent, that silences Pip.

Now the convict is in control, asking leading questions, dealing out his knowledge of Pip's affairs, one horrible fact at a time. Realization hits Pip so hard that he passes out, but he can't escape the truth; the man explains it eagerly now. He "made a gentleman" of Pip; he is Pip's "second father." From his story, we sense that his dream of making Pip rich was the one thing that kept him going for years. He pounces on

Pip's possessions, and offers to buy the "bright eyes" of Pip's love. Like Miss Havisham, gloating over Estella's beauty, festooning her with jewels, the convict feeds on his child selfishly, vengefully.

Then the convict reveals that if he's captured, he could be sentenced to death. Pip feels that the convict's unclean money is a burden; added to this now is the burden of protecting him from the law. Pip doesn't even love him, and yet he immediately shoulders the responsibility, feeding the old man, putting him to bed, as if he were the father and the convict his child. Consider why Pip does this. Some readers think he's acting out of guilt; others think he's being decent and kind. Which interpretation fits your image?

Alone, Pip sorts out his crushed dreams. He has lost his expectations of Miss Havisham's respectable fortune; he has lost his dreams of Estella; but worst of all, he has lost his real friendship with Joe. He almost seems to be lashing himself with regrets. "I could never, never, never, undo what I had done." As his anxiety mounts, irrational fears set in—fears for the convict, fear of the convict (after all, he's a violent criminal). Pip peeks at the sleeping man, his peaceful face at odds with the pistol on his pillow. Pip locks the door—to lock him in or lock others out?—then falls asleep. But when he awakens, the morning is still dark and dead, just like his expectations.

PART III

CHAPTER 40

As Part III begins, the novel shifts into a new mode, like a mystery. The need for action keeps Pip too busy to brood.

The plot thickens when, in the morning, Pip stumbles over someone sleeping on the staircase; he must run to fetch the watchman, search for the vanished intruder, question the watchman. Like a good detective, Pip gathers clues about the mysterious man who followed his visitor through the courtyard gate last night.

Next, Pip invents an alias for the convict—Uncle Provis—in case the servants ask questions. It's hard to get a grip on this character's identity. In daylight, let's take a better look at Abel Magwitch.

NOTE: In the Bible, Abel was Adam and Eve's good son, murdered by his brother Cain. If Magwitch were simply a criminal, Dickens would have named him Cain. Since he names him Abel instead, we should look for the man's goodness, and we should expect to see that he has been wronged by someone close to him. Keep this in mind as you learn his full story.

Last night Magwitch was a tragic, powerful figure; today he's a social embarrassment, with his bad table manners, his hoarse voice, his furrowed skull, his greasy black Bible. Yet whereas Pip's rooms intimidated Joe, Magwitch acts as if he owns them (he does, in fact). He wolfs down his food, smokes his pipe, flings his wallet onto the table, snaps his fingers. Try to see him in two lights at once: 1) as an uncouth figure that you'd be embarrassed to be seen with; and 2) as a self-confident survivor who has come to claim his due. He has enough dignity to sense when he's being "low"—not in Pip's sense ("coarse") but in his own sense ("less than noble"). Notice his calm courage about getting caught. He understands the danger, but he has lived through too much to cringe now.

Pip helps "Provis" work up a disguise; then he runs around the block to rent some rooms for him. Next he goes to Jaggers to verify what he has learned; isn't it natural to ask for extra proof before you can believe bad news? Jaggers is, as usual, cautious and verbally slippery; but for the first time Pip demands answers. Jaggers doesn't react to Pip's bitter disappointment, yet he's anxious for Pip not to blame him: he says he never led Pip to believe anything one way or another. Jaggers' intent look as Pip walks out suggests that he might, deep down, feel sorry for Pip—but that there's nothing he can do.

Magwitch's disguise, like Joe's Sunday clothes, only emphasizes the man's real nature. Dickens may be saying that what we wear outside isn't as important as who we are inside. Pip feels that Magwitch's dragging leg and savage air scream out his criminal identity, though he's so nervous that he probably imagines Magwitch looks worse than he does. Yet what is Magwitch really like inside? He seems ignorant and out of touch. His idea of a disguise—powdered hair and short breeches—was the style when he left England, but it looks ridiculous now. His manners are gross (worse than Joe's, for instance). He handles his jack-knife menacingly, and his slouching posture reminds us of bad men like Orlick or Drummle. Magwitch's crime is still a vague, horrible reality, too (typically, Pip can't bring himself to ask what it was, yet he tortures himself imagining it). But though Pip is physically scared of the man, he's also worried that Magwitch will be caught and killed just because he came home to see Pip. Again, a confused mixture of fear, conscience, and kindness join together in Pip's mind.

For five days, Pip is holed up with this man, feeling as if he has created a Frankenstein monster (this is a turnabout—Magwitch believes he "created" Pip). Finally Herbert comes home. Magwitch's threatening behavior towards Herbert, and Herbert's shocked reaction, prove to us that Pip isn't so wrong. Magwitch really poses a horrible problem.

CHAPTERS 41 & 42

In any society, different groups share different values and communicate in different languages. Here, Herbert and Pip are on one wavelength, and Magwitch on another. Magwitch is proud of what he has done for Pip. Yet after he has left, it's clear that Pip and Herbert regard the whole matter in a different light. They automatically assume that Pip shouldn't touch another penny of the old man's money. Herbert goes farther: Pip ought to pay back what he has already received.

NOTE: It's funny how the source of money defines its value for Pip and Herbert; no one minded Pip's accepting money from Miss Havisham. Dickens seems to disagree with their attitude. (Since both Pip and Herbert feel this way, Dickens is probably criticizing an attitude fairly common in his society.) Remember, Herbert has taken this money too, but as long as he doesn't realize it, he doesn't feel "tainted." Money itself isn't good or bad, it's what you do with it and how you feel about it that matters.

Pip now recognizes that a gentleman without money is a useless creature. But as gentlemen, Herbert and Pip try to treat Magwitch considerately, even though they're repelled by him. They realize that he must not be roughly rejected, or he might recklessly

turn himself in. They decide that Pip must get Magwitch safely abroad, before breaking his ties to the
man.

NOTE: Throughout this book, "being a gentleman" is
extremely important—but different people have different ideas of what it takes to be a gentleman. Consider these various marks of a gentleman: money,
stylish clothes, education, social graces, decent and
honorable behavior. Dickens himself seems to value
the last of these most highly, yet he realizes that, in
Pip's society, a man who lacks a good heart but has
money, or manners, or stylish clothes, may in fact get
treated like a gentleman. It's a slippery term. Watch
carefully how various characters—especially Pip—
use it.

The next morning, hoping to understand Magwitch
better, Pip and Herbert ask Magwitch to explain his
story. Chapter 42 is a long flashback told by Magwitch, who's an honest, unpretentious narrator.
Compare his life to his "son" Pip's. Magwitch knows
he was born to a life of crime. He had no parents (Pip
at least had the Gargerys) and he grew up like a wild
child, in one bad environment after another. His first
memory was of stealing turnips to keep himself alive.
(Pip's first memory is of stealing too—to help Magwitch.) All the authorities expected Magwitch to turn
out bad, and so he did. This is the most graphic example Dickens has yet given us of how a bad upbringing
can warp a child.

Then Magwitch met Compeyson—the convict Pip
saw him fighting that night Magwitch was recaptured. Magwitch's strongest impression of Compeyson was that he was a gentleman, and that he used
that fact to take advantage of others. (This explains

why Magwitch was so intent on making and owning a gentleman.) Compeyson had Magwitch do his dirty work, having already driven one accomplice, Arthur, into alcoholic despair. Magwitch relates dramatically how Arthur was haunted by the face of a rich lady they once swindled together. This should have warned Magwitch, but he seems not to have cared.

Compeyson was always able to manipulate Magwitch, tangling him more deeply in crime. Magwitch pauses emotionally, remembering a woman from his past, but he can't bring himself to tell about her now. (Notice—another fragment of mystery to be cleared up.) He goes on to describe how Compeyson turned on him when they were on trial, using his manners as a gentleman to get off lightly. Magwitch's simple dialect adds drama to his description of Compeyson's treachery.

Magwitch ends his tale with his battle with Compeyson on the marshes. Pip asks if Compeyson is dead (thinking, no doubt, of that suspicious figure on the stairs), but, ominously, Magwitch doesn't know. Meanwhile, Herbert casually pushes Pip a note, in which he adds his own startling knowledge: the alcoholic Arthur was Miss Havisham's brother, and the villainous Compeyson was the man who stood her up at the altar. The two worlds which Pip thought were so separate are in fact inextricably intertwined.

CHAPTERS 43 & 44

Recalling how the imaginary stain of Newgate weighed upon him, making him feel unworthy of Estella, Pip now feels that Magwitch's news absolutely divides him from Estella. Rather than dwell on this, Pip tries to concentrate on getting Magwitch away before Compeyson finds him. But Pip must face his duty to say goodbye to Miss Havisham and Estella before he goes abroad with Magwitch.

Events seem out of control. Estella is gone when he calls on her at Richmond, as though already she's slipping from his grasp. Following her to Rochester, Pip runs into Drummle at the inn. Like a pair of stubborn kids, they wage a silly duel over who shall stand closest to the fire (which seems to substitute for Estella). The situation will be familiar to anyone who has blown up a stupid argument just because he hated his opponent. Drummle is insolent and offensive, but Pip in his touchy pride isn't much better. The scene is almost entirely dialogue, as the two young men pit their wills against each other. People and details around them seem confused, as though Pip is too wrought-up to see them clearly. When Drummle finally rides away, Pip is reminded of Orlick. Pip heads for Satis House, unwillingly for once.

The gloomy ruin of the house fits Pip's spirits. He faces Miss Havisham and Estella, as he did Jaggers, grimly determined to know everything about his relation to them. But notice the kind of reaction Pip gets. Miss Havisham acts indifferent; she coolly admits that she led him on, but refuses to take responsibility for his pain. Estella sits silently, her fingers annoyingly busy with her knitting.

Pip presses on, doggedly. He reveals a second motive for this visit: to get Miss Havisham to help Herbert, now that Pip won't have any money to carry out his good deed. (Notice that Miss Havisham took false credit for being Pip's patron; Pip, in contrast, doesn't want to be known as Herbert's true patron.) But Miss Havisham turns a deaf ear. Then Pip clears up one last piece of business: he finally confesses his love for Estella. Everyone has taken it for granted for so long, and yet he has never been able to speak it

aloud. Estella seems anxious not to be blamed for
leading Pip on. She always warned him that she had
no heart; her obsessive fingers stop working only in
irritation that he hasn't accepted that yet. Notice how
all these characters—Estella, Jaggers, Miss Havisham—instead of sympathizing with Pip, focus immediately on themselves and the roles they played in
his disappointment. We see how selfish they are—
but Pip often behaves this way, too. Dickens may be
showing us that this is a common human trait.

Estella then tells Pip, haughtily, that she's going to
marry Drummle. This should be Miss Havisham's
moment of triumph, yet, as she hears Pip plead with
Estella not to throw herself away, the old lady looks
shaken. She never considered how Estella's victims
might feel; now her conscience smarts. Estella, however, remains emotionless, explaining her pragmatic
reasons for marrying Drummle.

The dialogue here is emotional, like a soap opera,
but somehow it isn't corny, it's effective. Pip ends
with a beautiful speech, summing up all his years of
love for Estella. (Notice Dickens' poetic effects, the
repetitions, the piled-up details, the parallel phrases.)
With a final cry of forgiveness, Pip rushes out. He
walks all the way back to London, trying to wear himself out so he can't feel anything.

But Pip can't dwell on his personal feelings; the plot
is moving ahead too fast. Wemmick has left a mysterious note for him at his lodgings gate warning him
not to go home.

CHAPTERS 45 & 46

Pip spends the night in a cheap, shady hotel called
the Hummums. In his anxiety and suspense, he imagines the room around him coming alive and attack-
ing him. Dickens describes Pip's hallucinations in

vivid detail, catching the peculiar feverish logic of nightmares.

Herbert's friendship has helped Pip with Magwitch; now Wemmick too comes through for him. The next day, at Walworth, Wemmick explains his warning note. He learned that Compeyson was closing in on Magwitch; Wemmick warned Herbert to hide the old man somewhere safe, and Herbert took him to stay with his fiancée Clara and her gruff old father. (We learn, in an embarrassed aside, that Pip has never met Clara because she disapproves of his influence on Herbert—another outsider's comment on Pip.) Although Wemmick claims to keep his personal and professional lives apart, he has gone against that policy here, using information from the office to help a friend. Though he's at Walworth, in explaining the case he talks in a parody of Jaggers' close-mouthed noncommittal style. Wemmick also hard-headedly advises Pip to lay hold of Magwitch's "portable property"; this seems more like a professional than a personal sentiment. Wemmick, with his Aged Parent, should sympathize instead with Pip's obligation to treat Magwitch kindly. But Wemmick mixes the two sides of his life now, in the name of friendship.

Clara's home is in an eccentric, out-of-the-way neighborhood. Seeing how much Herbert is at home there unsettles Pip, reminding him how little he knows of Herbert's life, but he doesn't brood over this, there's too much to do. Clara's drunken invalid father Bill Barley is an ogre, pounding and roaring overhead; he'd be far worse to live with than Wemmick's Aged Parent or even Magwitch. Clara, however, is patient with him. Pip's glad he has made things easier for her and Herbert; he seems to forget that Herbert's future has been paid for with tainted money, and may be lost.

In his rooms upstairs, "Provis" looks softer to Pip. Pip seems to have accepted Magwitch now. There may be several reasons for this: 1) Pip has finally given up his connection with Estella and Miss Havisham; 2) the danger Magwitch is in makes Pip pity him; 3) his better qualities are beginning to impress Pip. Pip handles Magwitch considerately, tactfully; he doesn't mention Compeyson for fear it will enrage him, and says nothing about his plans to break off with the man. In fact, Pip is already wondering if he shouldn't stick with him. Notice how Pip changes under the pressure of events. Watch Pip mature through a combination of factors: suffering, hard work, and human involvement.

NOTE: Magwitch, Provis, Campbell—the names seem interchangeable here. This may be because Pip's changing his feelings about who the man is. It may also say that the convict's a lost man, or that he's an ambiguous mixture of qualities, from a primitive world of murky values.

Pip is surprised at his own concern for Magwitch's safety. As Herbert and Pip discuss a plan for getting him down the river in a rowboat, the old man listens amiably, resting his fate completely in their hands. Back at their rooms, Herbert and Pip keep a lookout for the lurking figure shadowing Magwitch. The next morning Pip gets a rowboat and begins to establish himself as a regular on the river.

CHAPTERS 47 & 48

For weeks, Pip waits for Wemmick's signal to move Magwitch. Though he's hanging in suspense, the world around him doesn't stand still. His debts pile up, now that he won't use Magwitch's money (but notice that now he considers it a "heartless fraud" to take the money; before, he felt disgusted by it). He also senses that Estella's marriage is taking place somewhere, but he doesn't want to know for sure. To Pip's credit, his major worry during these weeks is about Magwitch. His waves of fear for the man's safety are like the river tides, which carry him back and forth past the house where Magwitch signals out of his window.

As he did in Chapter 31, Pip tries to forget his troubles by going to the theater. Dickens gives us a second burst of satire on the contemporary drama, making fun of cheap popular entertainments that were like bad musical comedy. As usual, Wopsle's ridiculous on stage, but he's also thrown off when he sees Pip in the audience. We can't quite sit back and just watch this play as we did the one before. After the play, Wopsle tells Pip that, sitting behind Pip, "like a ghost," Wopsle saw one of the two convicts from that long-ago battle on the marshes. Pip acts cool, but underneath he's shaken. This is no mere coincidence—just when he was forgetting his fears, Compeyson was right there following him! Danger and evil surround Pip, pervading everything. Pip deftly questions Wopsle, never giving away his urgent interest; then he goes home to tell Herbert and, via letter, Wemmick.

Coincidences and strange connections begin to multiply. Pip runs into Jaggers in the street, and is invited to dinner at Jaggers' house, where he's given a note from Miss Havisham. (Wemmick is there too, but around Jaggers he's like a different person, and Pip can't get any friendly response from him.) Jaggers seems to be trying to be sociable, but perhaps he doesn't know how. Jaggers brings up Estella's marriage, rather callously speculating on how Drummle will mistreat her. Just then, Pip is visited by another "ghost"—Estella's mysterious resemblance to someone—when Jaggers' housekeeper Molly walks in. Her knitting fingers, her intent eyes, her streaming hair—she has to be Estella's real mother! Pip's going on intuition, but he's convinced of the fact. Afterwards, walking homewards with Wemmick (who immediately becomes his private, friendly self), Pip asks another series of questions, to learn Molly's story. Wemmick tells him she was accused of murdering another woman in a fight over a man—Molly's common-law ("over the broomstick") husband. Jaggers, of course, got her acquitted. Part of his masterful defense revolved around Molly's little daughter, whom she reportedly killed to revenge herself on her faithless husband. It's a bloody tale of low-bred passion and violence—but, parting from Wemmick, Pip feels sure that Estella is that vanished daughter. Once again, the worlds of good and evil that he tried to keep pure and separate are tangled together.

CHAPTERS 49 & 50

Returning to Satis House, Pip sees it in a new light, as though he really is done with it. The old monastery with its monkish ghosts, the cathedral chimes and pealing organ, the cawing rooks, cast a funereal hush over the town, and Pip associates this with his dead dream of Estella. Estella's been replaced with a nondescript old woman at the gate of Satis House. Miss Havisham sits staring into an ashy fire (not a glowing fire, like Joe's). She's pitiful, shaky and vague. Ever since Pip's last visit, she has been brooding, blaming herself for his unhappiness. Pip, however, seems to have grown beyond her. He has other worries on his mind (Magwitch, no doubt), and he can freely forgive Miss Havisham now. In an amazing turnabout, Miss Havisham—who's always held power over Pip— kneels at his feet weeping. (Remember, Dickens has told us before that tears cleanse the soul.)

Pip shows surprising maturity in judging Miss Havisham. Rising above his own hurt, he concentrates on what she did to Estella, but he tries to see it in a sympathetic light. He notes that solitude is dangerous; only by becoming involved with other people can we get past our own vanities. If you think about it, Pip has just learned this lesson himself.

Miss Havisham's still a melodramatic figure, wailing "What have I done!" Pip acts like a practical man, giving her advice and asking about Estella's past. Having done what he planned—to help Herbert, to solve Estella's mystery—Pip leaves, knowing he can't be of any use in calming her.

But Pip hasn't turned into a dry realist. He's still romantic enough to wander around the grounds. He imagines Miss Havisham hanging from the beam again; instinct makes him go back to check if she's all right. He looks in her room; she bends over the fire, whoosh! she magically erupts into flame, as though all the stunted passion of her life has burst out.

Pip acts decisively, flinging his cloak over her. Then, in an ironic enactment of his old fairy-tale goals, he clears away the decaying bridal feast, but for a practical reason: so he can smother the fire with the tablecloth. Miss Havisham ends up, as she predicted, lying on the dining room table, covered in a white sheet. Although she lives, like Mrs. Joe she becomes dead for all intents and purposes once her spectacular energy is quenched.

It isn't until the next chapter that Pip tells us how
badly he was burned; he doesn't think his own inju-
ries are so important. Herbert, like a good friend,
changes Pip's bandages, doing it as tactfully as he
once corrected Pip's manners. Herbert agrees with
Pip that Magwitch gets nicer every day. Chatting to
pass the time, Herbert tells Pip another part of Magwitch's story—about that woman he couldn't talk
about before. Notice that this scene is straight dialogue, as if Pip is too tense to comment; only Herbert's
remarks show us how agitated Pip is. Pip does ask
brief, to-the-point questions, like a shrewd detective.
We, knowing what we do, can follow his reasoning.
This story is Molly's case, to the letter. Magwitch,
then, was the man she killed over, the man she
wanted to hurt by murdering his child. So, since
Molly is Estella's mother—Magwitch must be her
father. The most shining image of Pip's heart is mixed
up with his deepest fears and shame.

CHAPTERS 51 & 52

Just as Pip seemed beyond Miss Havisham's
power, now he seems to have grown beyond Jaggers'. Pip goes to Jaggers to get the truth about Estella,
though he can't separate whether he does this for love
of Estella, or of Magwitch. Jaggers is disappointed
that Pip got help for Herbert, and not for himself, out
of Miss Havisham. Wemmick professionally agrees.
Pip's above such selfish worries. Pip shocks the un-
shockable Jaggers by declaring he knows Estella's parents; the lawyer himself never knew Magwitch was
involved. Still, Jaggers evades Pip when he asks if it's
really true. Pip bursts into a heartfelt appeal—reminiscent of his confession of love for Estella—releasing
emotions he used to keep locked up inside.

When this doesn't work, Pip turns to Wemmick, appealing to Wemmick's "Walworth self" to plead with Jaggers. Pip is betraying a trust, but it breaks down barriers, and shows us surprising sides of Jaggers. Jaggers seems so pleased that Wemmick has human interests that, for once he releases information. His account of Molly's case shows compassion, in spite of the cautious, repeated phrase, "Put the case." Jaggers has seen a great deal of life; he feels moral outrage about children raised in evil environments (Magwitch's life story would support Jaggers' case). Wisely, Jaggers says that it won't do anyone any good to reunite Estella and her father now. And he suggests that he too has felt "poor dreams" of love in his time. It takes a special effort for Jaggers and Wemmick to restore their professional relations, but this has opened them up, in a good way.

Pip briskly finishes his business with Clarriker, to secure Herbert's partnership. Though he sadly learns that Herbert's being transferred to the Far East, Pip unselfishly feels consoled by Herbert's happiness. Herbert's the romantic one now, dreaming of caravans and camels.

Then the message from Wemmick comes, almost like a relief. Pip's gotten used to the idea of going with Magwitch, and doesn't seem to care where they go. Some readers think this shows Pip's self-sufficiency, that he can exist anywhere. Others say he faces this new life without hopes or expectations, afraid to be disappointed again; still others say it's just Pip's old vague manner.

Pip shows his new capacity for action. He and Herbert scurry around on their errands. Today's Monday; Wednesday they'll pick up Magwitch and take him down river to board a German steamship. The plot still twists, however. Going home, Pip finds an anon-

ymous note, demanding that he come secretly to the
marshes. Mostly because of the threat to "uncle Provis", Pip quickly makes up his mind to go. He's
changed a lot from the boy who couldn't decide
whether to run after Joe! This decision isn't necessarily
easy; Pip has a flurry of doubt, but by then he's already on the coach.

In an inn in Rochester, Pip ironically hears from the
innkeeper his own life story (the Pumblechook version, where Pip treated his "patron" with "ingrati-
tude"). Once Pip might have been offended by
Pumblechook's hypocrisy; now he feels humbled,
thinking how noble Joe is never to complain of Pip's
desertion. We've missed Joe lately—on Pip's recent
visits to Rochester, he didn't even think about stopping by Joe's. Pip has changed, but he still has a lot to
make up for.

CHAPTER 53

This dark night, with a red moon, creates a spooky
atmosphere, harking back to Compeyson and Magwitch's fight on the marsh. (The coming battle will
repeat that struggle, in a new generation.) The solitude seems ominous—we know that solitude's bad.
And worse than mists, we have thick ooze around the
lime-kiln, and a choking vapor in the air.

Pip describes the inside of the shed in objective
detail, like a police report. He's a rational figure—
suddenly hit by violence, pain, and darkness. Dickens
makes us feel how Pip feels. Yet Pip acts strong, concentrating not on his fears, but on noting the details of
his situation. A match is struck, revealing Orlick,
more satanic than ever.

Pip and Orlick's conversation is tensely dramatic:
quick speeches back and forth, mixed with threatening glimpses of powerful, vicious Orlick. Orlick's ha-

tred has festered in solitude. Everything boils together in his diseased mind; when he accuses Pip of coming between him "and a young woman I liked," it isn't clear at first whether it's Estella or Biddy, and it probably doesn't matter. Orlick—who speaks of himself as "Old Orlick," like a devil—has whipped up his own passions into uncontrollable rage.

Pip, his mind racing, imagines how people will react to his death—haven't we all thought about this?—but Pip mainly regrets that no one will know his good intentions. Some readers say this proves that he's a better person already; others say this is a moment of realization which will help him to reform. At any rate, Pip decides to survive. Pride is a good thing for once—it helps him to scorn and resist Orlick.

Orlick accuses Pip of murdering Mrs. Joe. Pip calmly replies that Orlick did it. Of course Pip isn't to blame if Orlick, feeling slighted by Pip, attacked her. That's crazy logic—though no crazier than when Pip felt responsible for the leg-iron. But Pip's outgrown that guilt. In contrast to Orlick's slow, muddled mind, Pip's rapid imagination flings up dozens of pictures. But you can't contrast these two so simply. Orlick's resourceful; clinging steadily to his revenge, he has been as good as Pip at dredging up information, solving the mystery of Magwitch. Orlick's home base, though, is a world of evil—it seems natural that he has linked up with Compeyson, like a kindred soul.

The dreadful suspense stretches out, as Orlick prepares to attack Pip; and Pip sees the scene like a slow-motion movie shot. Pip screams—it's a wild chance, knowing that they're so far out. But amazingly, a group of men burst in and rescue him. You may feel that this rescue is too easy: Pip happened to drop the

note, Herbert happened to pick it up and decided to
follow him out there. But it does suggest that friends
are crucial in "saving" our souls. Pip's done a good
deed for Herbert (though Herbert doesn't know it),
and Herbert, because he's fond of Pip, will put himself in danger for Pip.

NOTE: Trabb's Boy   Trabb's boy, of all people, helps
save Pip. Like Pip, he's growing up into a good, useful person. And it's a realistic change; he doesn't lose
his liveliness. Pip himself sees Trabb's boy in a new
light—as he's learning to do with many people
lately.

Orlick, like the essence of evil itself, escapes and
remains at large. But Pip doesn't press charges
because it would delay him in helping Magwitch
escape; helping someone is more important to him
than getting revenge. He goes home with Herbert,
sick and restless with pain. But the sparkling day-
break at the end of the chapter is—we hope—a good
omen.

CHAPTER 54

Action is a relief to Pip, as he, Herbert, and their
friend Startop set out on the river that morning. Pip
pauses for a second to wonder what his future will
bring; but as long as he can save Magwitch, he'll go
anywhere.

Dickens' description of the Thames River is accu-
rate and detailed. The water is crowded with boats,
full of life. In the open air and sunlight, everything
looks safe, though Pip keeps a wary lookout. He's
pleased, now, with the way Magwitch looks when
they pick him up, and observes only good things
about him. Has Magwitch changed, or has Pip

changed? Probably both. Magwitch seems more contented and peaceful than before—perhaps because he has found his "son." He faces danger philosophically, though he loves freedom. Trailing his hand in the water, he profoundly compares the river to life: mysterious and swiftly flowing. He, like Jaggers, has acquired wisdom from life.

Like life, the river is changeable. After the tide turns, the mood shifts from hope to tragedy. The landscape becomes flat, like the marshes; the river's sluggish, there are no other boats around. They can't see above the muddy banks, and Herbert and Startop have to row hard. Suspicion, dread, and silence settle upon them. They stop for the night at a dirty, disreputable inn. The Jack (odd-job man), a slimy scavenger who robs drowned corpses, makes them uneasy with his talk about a boat with four men in it that has been hanging around. To the Jack, the boat is ominous because it could belong to Customs Officers, hunting smugglers. But Pip's scared of the law, too—as well as of the outlaw Compeyson. Legal and illegal are blurred in his mind; so are right and wrong.

The sense of danger deepens when Pip sees two men looking at his boat in the middle of the night. But Pip meets this danger briskly, with a plan where he and Magwitch will meet the boat down shore, to avoid being seen. Pip rushed into danger with Orlick, but now that Magwitch is in his care, he's cautious. His language is clear and businesslike as he follows each step of the action next morning.

Orlick's attack was dark, sudden, and melodramatic, but this daytime scene is underplayed, in a sort of numb, silent, slow motion. The German ship steams head on towards the little boat. Another rowboat appears out of nowhere. There's no dialogue, except for the police officer's inevitable call of arrest.

No one seems to control the rowboats, and the steamer's too big to maneuver. Collision is unavoidable. Imagine Pip sitting in the boat, watching two kinds of calamity approach, helpless to prevent either one.

Magwitch rises to action, though. Immediately recognizing the cloaked figure in the other boat, he ignores danger and goes after his enemy. Only Magwitch understands what's going on: Compeyson turned the police onto their trail, using the law for his own unlawful ends. (Good and evil are mixed again.)

What happens next is confusing. Both Magwitch and Compeyson go overboard and under the steamer; only Magwitch surfaces. Did he drown Compeyson? Magwitch says he didn't, though he would have liked to. Pip tells us Magwitch's account was never doubted, leaving us to wonder.

But though this mystery remains forever unsolved, Pip's uncertainty about his relationship to Magwitch is settled. Especially now, with Magwitch injured and in handcuffs, Pip sees him in the most sympathetic light, valuing his loyalty and love. Even Magwitch sees that it would be better for Pip not to be associated with him, but Pip won't desert him. Holding Magwitch's hand on his way back to jail, Pip puts himself publicly on the line for the old convict.

CHAPTERS 55 & 56

Pip fills us in on the details of Magwitch's case. Jaggers says it's open-and-shut. Even Magwitch's money will be lost, since a felon's property is usually turned over to the state. Pip, however, won't let himself get caught up in chasing after money anymore.

Pip quietly accepts responsibility for Magwitch, just as he accepts Herbert's news that he must go to his new job in the East. Now that we're reaching the final chapters, loose ends of the plot are being tied up. Herbert's going to marry Clara soon (and she now approves of Pip—a good sign). Herbert also offers Pip a job, which proves that good deeds do eventually pay off. But Pip won't take the job yet. Why not? Pip's changed, but maybe he doesn't feel ready yet to start a new life. More suffering and repentance lie ahead for him. As you read, consider: Is this Pip's own hang-up, that he must pay for his sins? Or does Dickens himself believe that people have to suffer before they can be happy?

Wemmick stops by to clear up the last facts of the case for Pip and, personally of course, to say he's sorry Magwitch was caught.

NOTE: Wemmick, like Jaggers, still regrets that Pip lost Magwitch's money. This obsession tells us something about these particular men's values. But they may have a point; money can be useful. Dickens may be reminding us that money is important, and, in our world, it would be naïve to pretend otherwise.

We shift into exaggerated comedy again for Wemmick's wedding-day. Wemmick pretends that he's doing all this on the spur of the moment, that he just happened to pass a church and Miss Skiffins and the Aged P just happened to be there. This isn't a very romantic wedding, and though we may laugh at Wemmick's light-hearted attitude, it seems overdone. This wedding shows that love doesn't have to be as serious as Pip thinks. But on the other hand, when you see Miss Skiffins sitting primly in her chair, allowing Wemmick's arm to stay around her waist at last, can you imagine Pip ever being content with this kind of love, either?

The next chapter shifts back into melodrama. Lying ill in prison, Magwitch seems transformed into a humble angel—in ironic contrast to his reputation as a desperate criminal. Again, we realize that it's not so easy to sum up any human being as good or bad.

Sentimental and melodramatic as this chapter is, we must remember that Dickens takes it absolutely seriously. He sets the scene where Magwitch is sentenced to death as if he were painting a huge, historical painting, full of characters. The shaft of sunlight slants effectively across the courtroom, linking judge and prisoners. Like a formal painting, it gives a special dignity to the focal figure, Magwitch. Other people are glimpsed in still poses, not in action; we hear no dialogue, except for Magwitch's moving speech to the judge.

Dickens is serious in putting God above mortal authority. He says God sends death to Magwitch as a merciful sign of forgiveness, in contrast to society's harsh execution. After the sentence, Pip never gives up, remaining active in Magwitch's behalf until the bitter end. Magwitch, in contrast, seems at peace, far from the troubles of this world (another sign that God has forgiven him).

Magwitch's death scene is moving, drawn out to full tear-wrenching effect. Yet it isn't emotional; Pip and Magwitch scarcely move, and they speak to each other in brief, simple speeches. There's not much left to say—except for one thing. In spite of Jaggers' shrewd advice, Pip tells Magwitch about Estella, kindly setting the old man's heart at rest. The chapter ends with a Biblical reference to the parable of the pious Pharisee and the publican (*Luke* 18:10–14.), a story which illustrates God's forgiveness of repentant sinners like Magwitch.

CHAPTER 57

Pip is truly on his own—not just solitary but abandoned, facing life's struggles alone. Like many people after a period of great stress, he physically collapses. On top of this, he's arrested for debt (he only escapes jail because he's so sick). Pip may have changed, but he still has to pay for the past.

Dickens, as we've seen before, loves to describe disordered states of mind. He shows us how Pip, in his brain fever, jumbles together real and imaginary, past and present. Whereas at the Hummums Pip imagined objects coming alive, now he imagines that he's turning into an object, imprisoned in the shape of a brick or a steel beam. Dickens is a shrewd psychologist (even before psychology became a science!), and he makes Pip's ravings all symbolize some anxiety. He relives terrors linked with Miss Havisham and Orlick, and he imagines struggling with murderers, figures resembling Magwitch, who always turn out to be good. When Pip sees Joe's face over and over, it's like another hallucination, rising out of guilt.

It isn't: it really is Joe. Notice that Joe was gone from the book the whole time Magwitch was with Pip; as Joe returns, he seems for a moment like a version of Magwitch, sitting in the window, smoking a pipe. Both were like fathers to Pip, and he treated both unfairly. But Magwitch was an intense figure, either evil or noble, speaking with his own eloquence: Joe is simpler, and speaks in his old inarticulate, muddled way. Like Pip, we feel delighted to hear him again; it feels like coming home.

Though Joe is his old self, life hasn't stood still waiting for Pip. Biddy has taught Joe to write (doing for love what Pip couldn't do for mere ambition). More strands of the plot are tied up, as Joe tells Pip of Miss Havisham's death, and the "coddleshells" (codicils) of her will. Our final view of her shows power and wilful intelligence, as she doles out fitting legacies to all the Pockets (Matthew has been rewarded because of Pip—another good deed done). Joe also brings news of Pumblechook and Orlick: Orlick broke into Pumblechook's house, robbed him, and humiliated him. Orlick has since been caught and put in jail. Two very different "villains" are both punished here, in one stroke.

Joe and Pip enjoy another Sunday outing, though Pip, still weak, seems a child again; Joe has to carry him. The mood is one of peace and renewal. But you can never undo the past. When Pip tries to explain to Joe about Magwitch, Joe doesn't want to hear it; it involves too many complicated memories—of Pip stealing from the pantry, of Mrs. Joe beating the boy and Joe unable to protect him. Joe shows a complex understanding here, but it isn't all his own wisdom; Biddy helped him see it. Pip isn't jealous of her and Joe, but we should begin to suspect something.

This peace can't last forever; Joe becomes more and more uncomfortable, until one morning he's gone, having paid off Pip's debts. Pip looks a little bit like a silly snob again for his complicated pride about this money. Pip isn't fully reformed yet; he's still blind to certain human truths. With all good intentions, he heads for the old village, determined to make up with Biddy, marry her, and live near Joe. He feels pleased with himself for doing this. Pip still has a lesson or two to learn.

CHAPTERS 58 & 59

Returning to Rochester, Pip finds all his old dreams dismantled. At the hotel, he's treated like a nobody because he isn't rich anymore. Satis House is all marked up and pulled apart in preparation for an auction. Pumblechook tracks Pip down so he can patronize him in his misfortune.

At first, Pip puts up with Pumblechook with the same sort of quiet resignation he has shown towards the other changes. But Pumblechook's air of pity and condescension is too much for Pip. Watch how his irritation grows, until finally he bursts out rudely. Pumblechook brings up too many sore memories: how badly Pip treated Joe, how much more loving Pip's real benefactor Magwitch was. Pip's reaction may show: 1) he's still not completely reformed; 2) he's reformed, but he's still got enough spirit to resent a gross hypocrite like Pumblechook; or 3) his scorn and impatience will always be a part of him; he's learning to control them, but he'll never be perfect.

Pip escapes into the healthier climate of the spring countryside, which reflects his regenerated spirit. But as Magwitch pointed out, life's a river that keeps on flowing. Pip presumes he can pick up with these people where he left them. He's first disappointed that Biddy's not in her schoolhouse; next he's surprised to find Joe's forge quiet and empty. Then he sees Joe and Biddy and learns they've just gotten married. Just as with Herbert, Pip's been too selfish to notice the hints about their relationship. Now, in a turnabout of the day Pip learned about his expectations, Joe and Biddy have good news and Pip has to pretend to be happy for them. He generously wishes them well, but he immediately decides to leave the country and take the job with Herbert. How do you think Pip is feeling? Your answer will depend in part on whether you think he really loves Biddy. Some readers think his heart's broken, and he's running away from it. Others say it's only his pride that has been hurt, and he's trying to save face. And still others say he goes away because he still has to suffer more to earn happiness.

Now we leap ahead eleven years. Pip summarizes what's happened to him: he has learned to work hard and to be content with a modest but honest living, and he has become partners with Herbert and Clarriker. Finally returning to England, he visits Joe and Biddy. He seems resigned, content to treat Biddy and Joe's son as his "son." The mood is melancholy, reminiscent of the December evening in the graveyard where we began. But though Pip tells Biddy that he has accepted his role as an old bachelor, he's not entirely convincing. He feels Biddy's wedding-ring when he squeezes her hand. She asks about Estella, and he falters when he says he has gotten over her.

At this point, Dickens originally wrote a different ending. In this first version, Pip learns that Drummle treated Estella badly, but he died, and she then married a country doctor who treated her better. Pip runs into her in London, where he gathers that she has grown to have a heart and regrets how she treated him. On the advice of a fellow writer, Dickens changed that ending.

In the final version—the one you have—that night Pip slips away from Joe and Biddy to go gaze nostalgically at where Satis House used to stand. He has heard that Estella was unhappy with Drummle, but that he recently died. By coincidence (or fate), Estella is walking in the old ruined garden that evening too.

The scene is misty and moonlit (symbolizing Pip's romantic, unrealistic side) but the stars (symbolizing Estella) shine clear. Pip notices that Estella has changed—she is still beautiful, but softened by sadness. There's a quiet, restrained tone to their conversation. The melodrama that used to surround Estella in Pip's eyes is gone now, replaced by a realistic view of a human being.

Pip's final line is, "I saw no shadow of another parting from her"—meaning that there were no longer any barriers to their getting together. But that line appeared only when the novel was published in book form. In the magazine serial version, he says, "I saw the shadow of no parting from her"—which could be interpreted to mean that they would get together for a while, but later they would break up. Just a word or two are different, but they significantly change the feeling of the ending.

Which of these endings do you prefer?

1.   Some readers have said that Dickens' first version is more believable, because Pip is melancholy by nature and ought to end up alone. They add that Estella has been so rotten to him that the only happy ending is one where he escapes from her influence.

2.   Others like the magazine serial version, because it shows that Pip is still romantic Pip, falling for Estella, but Estella is still Estella too, and will someday break his heart again. These readers believe that Dickens saw life as an endless path of suffering, with no real happy endings.

3.   Others prefer the final version—not just because it's happy but because it fits. They believe Dickens' message is that people learn from suffering; Estella, like Pip, has reformed and now they deserve

happiness. These readers add that Dickens has shown us it's good to forge ties to other people, so we shouldn't want Pip to be solitary all his life.

Which ending is more satisfying? Which is more realistic? The ongoing debate over this question just proves what a rich, complex novel this is.

A STEP BEYOND

Tests and Answers

TESTS

Test 1

1. The escaped convict sent Pip for _____
   A. a file and some "wittles"
   B. a spy glass and his dad's hunting gun
   C. "the Tickler"

2. Pip and Joe are seen as suffering from _____
   A. the isolation of the marsh country
   B. Mrs. Gargery's violent temper
   C. the sharp criticism of hypocritical neighbors

3. In his first meeting with Estella, Pip _____
   A. proposed marriage to her
   B. vowed to discover her secret
   C. was made to feel ashamed of his upbringing

4. At the Three Jolly Bargemen, a stranger _____
   A. stirred his drink with a file
   B. showed Pip a rusted set of leg irons
   C. taped a pound note to the underside of Pip's plate

5. As he continues to visit Miss Havisham, Pip _____
   I. begins to develop feelings about social class
   II. reveals feelings of inferiority
   III. determines to improve his position in the world

A. I and II only   B. II and III only
C. I, II, and III

6. Biddy enters Pip's home as a direct result of _____
   A. Pip's "great expectations"
   B. the prisoner's escaped from Hulks
   C. the attack on Mrs. Joe

7. Herbert Pocket's nickname for Pip is _____
   A. Mr. Smith
   B. Handel
   C. Born Again

8. "He seemed to bully his very sandwich as _____
   he ate it" is Dickens' comment on
   A. Mr. Jaggers
   B. Uncle Pumblechook
   C. Bentley Drummle

9. "Portable property" is _____
   A. Jaggers' plaster casts
   B. Wemmick's jewelry
   C. Wopsle's stage gear

10. Wemmick shot off a cannon each night to _____
    A. frighten away the thieves
    B. give his deaf father something to hear
    C. leave the office behind

11. Discuss the theme of snobbery in this novel.

12. What is this book's definition of a gentleman?

Test 2

1. Jaggers mysteriously calls attention to _____
   A. Wemmick's pocket watch
   B. Molly's scarred wrist
   C. Drummle's handwriting

2. When Joe visits London, Pip _____
   A. renews their friendship with gusto

B. realizes the common man's superiority

C. fears being ridiculed by Drummle

3. "It's me wot has done it!" is spoken to Pip _____
by

    A. his brother-in-law, Joe Gargery

    B. his benefactor, Abel Magwitch

    C. his nemesis, Orlick

4. Which of these matchups is incorrect? _____

    A. Pip—Philip Pirrip

    B. Compeyson—Bill Barley

    C. Provis—Campbell

5. Estella's mother _____

    A. terrified Miss Havisham into adopting
       the little girl

    B. was saved from the hangman by Jaggers

    C. secretly wanted Pip to marry her
       daughter

6. Miss Havisham urged Pip to write _____

    A. "I forgive her"

    B. "She died of a broken heart"

    C. "All beauty is vanity"

7. Both Pip and his sister were victims of _____

    A. Orlick

    B. Jaggers

    C. Compeyson

8. Without hopes of "great expectations," Pip _____

    A. has to break his engagement to Estella

    B. is depressed yet elated

    C. behaves in a more decent fashion

9. Dickens' theme may be stated as _____

    A. true goodness does not depend upon
       wealth or social status

    B. good deeds are their own reward

    C. you cannot tell a book by its cover

10. The ending of the book is noteworthy because
    A. it contains the same words as the opening sentence
    B. it differed sharply from other Victorian novels
    C. Dickens wrote it two different ways

11. Discuss the river as a symbol of life.

12. Discuss the importance of friendship in this novel.

ANSWERS

Test 1

1. A   2. B   3. C   4. A   5. C   6. C

7. B   8. A   9. B   10. B

11. There are two ways you could answer this question.

First, you can look at the main character, Pip, as a prototype of The Snob. Discuss the various elements in his personality that cause him to become a snob. Then examine a particular scene or two where Pip behaves like a snob, and discuss how the reader is meant to feel about Pip at this point. Finally, talk about how Pip reforms, and why.

Another way to answer would be to look at many different snobs throughout the book. You couldn't do any of them in depth, but you could show how many different forms snobbery takes in this novel. For instance, there are the social snobs: Pip, Estella, Mrs. Pocket, Herbert, and even Magwitch, who longs to "own" a gentleman. They believe that social position and manners are everything. Next there are the money snobs—Pumblechook, Mrs. Joe, the greedy Pockets—as well as the tradesmen and servants who take advantage of rich people. They fawn on anyone who has money. Finally, there are the moral snobs: Biddy and Jaggers. They look down harshly on anybody who doesn't behave right morally. Devote a paragraph to each type of snobbery, and give examples of how each of these characters acts out his or her particular snobbery. Then, in your final paragraph, discuss the total effect of having so many types of snobs in this fictional world.

12. Before you begin answering, list on another piece of paper all the different characters who could be considered gentlemen. Don't forget the gentlemen villains, like Compeyson and Drummle, or the natural gentlemen, like Joe. Then list several qualities which distinguish a gentleman in this book, such as money, education, manners, or honorable behavior.

Then you can structure your answer in one of two ways.

You could discuss the gentlemen in the book one by one, arranging them in order from good to bad, or from true to false. End with a paragraph summing up what you think Dickens is saying about his society by showing so many different types of gentlemen.

Or you could discuss what you think is Dickens' ideal gentleman, one quality at a time. Illustrate each quality with examples of characters from the book, the good as well as the bad. Your final paragraph should then sum up Dickens' ideal gentleman.

Test 2

1. B   **2.** C   **3.** B   **4.** B   **5.** B   **6.** A

7. A   **8.** C   **9.** A   **10.** C

11. In your first paragraph, describe the scene on the river where Magwitch compares the river to life. Explain what's happening in the book at this point. Then briefly interpret what Magwitch says.

Go on to discuss other scenes in which the river appears, and relate them to Magwitch's metaphor. Then expand the metaphor even farther. Talk about life in general as it appears in this book. How does it support Magwitch's comparison?

12. First, jot down a list of various friendships. Most of these will probably be Pip plus somebody else, like Joe or Herbert or Wemmick, but add any others you think of. Put a star next to the good friendships, and an arrow by the bad ones.

Then you can structure your answer in two different ways.

You can discuss all the good friendships first, and then all the bad ones. Wrap up your discussion by talking about how friends affect the plot and illustrate certain themes of the novel.

Or, since Pip is the main character, you could discuss Pip's friendships first, and then other friendships. Then you would wrap up this discussion by explaining what Pip learns about friendship, and how other friendships in the book relate to that.

Whichever way you choose to answer this question, be sure you talk about specific deeds of friendship, such as Pip trying to teach Joe how to read, or Herbert rescuing Pip, or Compeyson and Arthur Havisham scheming together to swindle Miss Havisham. End by telling your readers how you feel about these deeds.

Term Paper Ideas

1. Discuss the theme of revenge. Which characters seek revenge, and why? How do you think Dickens regards revenge?

2. Discuss the theme of forgiveness. Which characters show forgiveness naturally, and which have to learn it? Why is forgiveness important in this book?

3. Discuss the theme of education. Compare Pip's various teachers and discuss how Joe learns to read and write. What does Pip want in an education? What value do you think Dickens places on it?

4. Discuss one character other than Pip who has "great expectations." Compare that character's fate to Pip's.

5. Look at each of Pip's "fathers"—Joe, Jaggers, Magwitch, and Pumblechook. What does each offer him? What does each lack?

6. Compare the three orphans, Pip, Biddy, and Estella. How are they alike? How are they different?

7. Compare Bentley Drummle and Pip.

8. What scene do you think shows Pip at his worst? Discuss in detail how Dickens shows Pip as a flawed human being.

9. Compare Miss Havisham and Magwitch, as patrons, as parents, and as seekers of revenge.

10. Compare and contrast Mrs. Joe and Mrs. Matthew Pocket, as mothers and as women.

Further Reading

CRITICAL WORKS

Biographies

Forster, John. *The Life of Charles Dickens,* 2 volumes (London: S.M. Dent & Sons, 1872–1874).

Johnson, Edgar. *Charles Dickens, His Tragedy and Triumph,* Volumes 1 and 2 (New York: Simon & Schuster, 1952).

Wilson, Angus. *The World of Charles Dickens* (New York: Viking Press, 1970).

General Criticism

Carey, John. *The Violent Effigy* (London: Faber & Faber, 1973).

Chesterton, G.K. *Charles Dickens* (New York: Schocken Books, 1965).

Fielding, K.J. *Charles Dickens: A Critical Introduction* (New York: Longman, 1958).

Ford, George H., and **Lauriat Lane,** editors. *The Dickens Critic* (Ithaca, New York: Cornell University Press, 1961).

Gissing, George. *Dickens, A Critical Study* (New York: Haskell House, repr 1965).

Gross, John, and **Gabriel Pearson,** editors. *Dickens and the Twentieth Century* (London: Routledge & Kegan Paul, 1962).

House, Humphrey. *The Dickens World* (London: Oxford University Press, 1941).

Maurois, André. *Dickens.* Translated by Hamish Miles (New York: J. Lane, 1934).

Price, Martin, editor. *Dickens: A Collection of Critical Essays* (Englewood Cliffs, New Jersey: Prentice-Hall, 1967).

Wilson, Edmund. *The Wound and the Bow* (Boston: Houghton-Mifflin, 1941).

Zabel, Morton Dauwen. *Craft and Character* (New York: Viking Press, 1957).

AUTHOR'S OTHER WORKS

Sketches by Boz. 1834–36.

Pickwick Papers. 1836–37.

Oliver Twist. 1837.

Nicholas Nickleby. 1838–39.

The Old Curiosity Shop. 1840–41.

Barnaby Rudge. 1841.

Martin Chuzzlewit. 1843–44.

A Christmas Carol. 1843.

Dombey and Son. 1846–48.

David Copperfield. 1849–50.

Bleak House. 1852–53.

Hard Times. 1854.

Little Dorrit. 1855–57.

A Tale of Two Cities. 1859.

Our Mutual Friend. 1864–65.

The Mystery of Edwin Drood. 1870.

Glossary

Argus A King of Greece who had a hundred eyes, and only closed two at a time to sleep.

Ballast-lighters Barges that carried gravel or sand to sailing ships, to weigh them down if they had no cargo.

Barnard's Inn Originally, one of the Inns of Chancery, a series of buildings around courtyards where lawyers lived and studied. However, by this time Barnard's was no longer a place to study law.

Battery A place where artillery guns were set up. Dickens is referring to the old battery at Cliffe Creek, which was a ruin.

Bed-furniture The cloth draperies around an old four-poster bed.

Blacking Ware'us The shoe polish factory where Dickens worked as a boy. He probably stuck this in as a private joke.

Botany Bay The port in Australia where transported convicts were delivered.

Bridewells A famous prison at Bridewell was torn down in 1863. Bridewell became a slang term meaning any prison.

Britannia metal A cheap alloy which looks like silver if it's polished.

Calendar The Newgate Calendar, a five-volume collection of biographies of famous criminals.

'Change The Royal Exchange, where the merchants' insurance company, Lloyd's of London, had its offices.

Coal-whippers Men who helped load coal into barges.

Commercials Travelling salesmen.

Covent Garden An area of London, near the Opera House and the fruit-and-flower markets, which was in Dickens' time known for prostitution.

Crib Slang for a place to shelter.

Cut A deliberate social snub.

Double Gloucester A cheese which is made in especially big blocks.

Flip A punch mixed of beer, liquor, and sugar, stirred with a hot poker.

Fluey Fluffy or dusty.

Grinder A private tutor for rich men's sons.

Hammercloth A cloth covering the coachman's seat.

Hardback Almond toffee.

Hulks Old ships used to hold convicts who were scheduled to be transported.

Jack-towel A roller towel.

Jorum A big punch bowl, or metaphorically a vast amount of any drink.

Little Britain A street near St. Paul's Cathedral and the law courts, running past the site of the ancient home of the Duke of Brittany. By using this name, Dickens suggests that this place is a microcosm of Britain.

Lloyd's The great merchants' insurance company.

Mentor The wise old companion of Ulysses' son, Telemachus, in the *Odyssey*.

Mitre The headgear of a bishop.

Newgate Prison One of the great prisons of London.

Physic A medicine, often a strong laxative.

Quintin Matsys A great Flemish painter who was first a blacksmith.

Rantipole A slang nickname for Napoleon III of France. The name means "raving head."

Red book A guide-book to all the nobility of England.

Repeater A pocket-watch that strikes the hour.

Rope-walk A long alley, usually under a roof, where rope was made.

Roscian Resembling a famous Roman actor, written about by Cicero.

Rush-light A crude, low-cost candle made of reeds dipped in grease.

Shake-down A rough sort of cot.

Shorts Tight knee-breeches.

Slop suit A sailor's outfit.

Swab A slang term for sailor.

Tar-water A mixture of cold water and wood tar, which was thought to have medical powers.

Telemachus Ulysses' son in the *Odyssey*.

Thowels Wooden pins used as oarlocks.

verb. sap. A Latin abbreviation meaning "a word to the wise."

Weazen Slang for throat.

Whitlow A red, swollen, sore place around a finger or toe nail.

Winding-sheets Shrouds.

Woolsack The seat of a high court judge or the Lord Chancellor of England.

The Critics

"Dickens . . . was . . . the greatest dramatic writer that the English had had since Shakespeare, and he created the largest and most varied world." (Edmund Wilson)

"I do not for a moment maintain that [Dickens] enjoyed everybody in his daily life. But he enjoyed everybody in his books. . . . His books are full of baffled villains stalking out or cowardly bullies kicked downstairs. But the villains and the cowards are such delightful people that the reader always hopes the villain will put his head through a side window and make a last remark; or that the bully will say one more thing, even from the bottom of the stairs." (G.K. Chesterton)

"When (Dickens) aims at depicting the simply good, the touchingly ingenuous, he is never so successful as with the amusingly base; and this has its cause in the nature of things, for the society with which he is concerned does not favour goodness and ingenuousness . . . there goes on a furious struggle for existence, and assuredly the self-forgetful do not win the fight." (George Gissing)

"Perhaps, properly speaking, [Dickens] had no *ideas* on any subject; what he had was a vast sympathetic participation in the daily life of mankind; and what he saw of ancient institutions made him hate them, as needless sources of oppression, misery, selfishness, and rancour." (George Santayana)

"That Dickens was a great genius and is permanently among the classics is certain. But the genius was that of a great entertainer, and he had for the most part no profounder responsibility as a creative artist than this description suggests." (F.R. Leavis)

"(Dickens) is always preaching a sermon, and that is the final secret of his inventiveness. For you can only create if you can *care*." (George Orwell)

"When (Dickens) imagined a street, a house, a room, a figure, he saw it not in the vague schematic way of ordinary imagination, but in the sharp definition of actual perception, all the salient details obtruding themselves on his attention. He, seeing it thus vividly, made us also see it." (George Henry Lewes)

"Dickens' London may be different from actual London, but it is just as real, its streets are of firm brick, its inhabitants genuine flesh and blood. . . . It does not matter that Dickens' world is not lifelike: it is alive." (David Cecil)

"[In *Great Expectations*] the comedy makes the serious elements stand out. It gives relief. The humorous chapters do not simply alternate with serious ones; the strands of comedy and tragedy are closely interwoven. . . . It is the fundamental irony of the book that makes this possible from the start: the fact that it was tragi-comic in its initial conception." (K.J. Fielding)